A FLAT WORLD WITH FLAGS ON

Louise Rivenell

MINERVA PRESS
MONTREUX LONDON WASHINGTON

ISBN 1 85863 902 6

First published 1996 by
MINERVA PRESS
195 Knightsbridge
London SW7 1RE

Printed in Great Britain by
Antony Rowe Ltd., Chippenham, Wiltshire

A FLAT WORLD WITH FLAGS ON

*With grateful thanks to Santie,
who provided the photographs
and to Pinney
for her help and encouragement.*

CONTENTS

	Page
Chapter One	9
Chapter Two	11
Chapter Three	17
Chapter Four	24
Chapter Five	33
Chapter Six	45
Chapter Seven	58
Chapter Eight	68
Chapter Nine	81
Chapter Ten	92

Chapter Eleven 102

Chapter Twelve 110

Chapter Thirteen 122

Chapter Fourteen 130

Chapter Fifteen 141

Chapter Sixteen 154

Chapter Seventeen 167

Chapter Eighteen 178

Chapter Nineteen 189

Chapter Twenty 194

LIST OF ILLUSTRATIONS

1. "TO GRACE, FROM MAY"

2. AUNTY'S HOUSE

3. AUNTY MAY AND UNCLE FRED

4. SOCKLESS IN TORQUAY

5. OFF TO NEWTON MARKET

6. "A BIT OF A BLOW"

7. THE LITTLE FAIRY

8. NO CAT CALLS TODAY

9. "THIS ONE'S FOR MUMMY"

10. UNCLE FRED'S PICNIC SUIT

11. THE COVETED IVORY BUCKLE

12. AUNTY MAY BY THE VILLAGE POND

13. "TO MAY, FROM GRACE"

Chapter One

"I wouldn't be a bit surprised," said my mother, "if May went over to Rome."

Where was Rome? Was it further than Torquay? Aunty May always took my sister and me everywhere with her but our coats hadn't been got out (loud coat-hanger rattling in the spare room wardrobe was a sure sign of going out). Worrying that she might go without us, I sidled up and asked,

"Where's Rome?"

I had just learnt to read and not understanding my question she lifted me up to the big old wireless and pointed out the word R O M E on its fretworked face.

"There it is, Pieface," she said. "Now be a very good girl, keep nice and clean and we'll all go to Dawlish this afternoon."

It was Wartime, barbed wire on the red sandy seafront so you couldn't play on the beach. Our special treat was a lovely teashop which sold little cakes made from cocoa powder and cornflakes. I adored them. The nice lady always said,

"I know what the little maid'll want, don' I?" My sister Santie, being nearly eleven, was far too sophisticated for such a sticky treat and ate 'grown up' food and drank a cup of tea with her white gloves on.

Santie and I lived with Aunty May, Uncle Fred, Gramps and Ginger, a marmalade cat with six toes on her front paws. An assortment of chickens, ducks and rabbits came – and went (mostly into stews) – although the chickens stayed a few years as egg suppliers. The ducks were a short-lived scheme as the nearest pond was in our next door neighbour's paddock, where Penny the pony lived. The ducks had to be shooed quacking down the path from their pen at the top of our garden, up the step into the little grassy 'arbour' (damp green wooden seat and bird table), through the hedge into the field, where they spotted the water and fled from us.

These tiresome manoeuvres proved too much both for us and the ducks so they remained next door and that was that. Mrs A passed over their eggs from time to time for whenever Aunty would "fancy a nice duck egg for tea" one miraculously appeared.

"Too strong for you two, you wouldn't like it, but try a bit anyway." She was right of course, we spat it out.

Mum and Dad stayed on in South London 'for the duration' as it was called. I think my mother was secretly rather pleased not to have us about all the time because she could give her full attention to Dad, who did not enjoy very good health. Anyway, she was not overly maternal at the best of times although she jealously guarded her rights in us.

"After all, May," I'd hear her saying on one of their infrequent weekend visits, "they are *my* children when all's said and done. I think I have *some* say in their upbringing even if you don't."

Then back they'd go to London and Santie and I carried on exactly as before this intrusion, loved and cared for. Aunty's easily ruffled feathers soon smoothed down for with Mum and Dad out of the way we were again her very own little girls.

Chapter Two

It was the Easter holidays, bright, sunny and breezy. By some mysterious negotiations on Santie's part we were allowed to go to Torquay one afternoon on our own. Got ready with coat and gloves on, told to "keep clean like a good little girl," I sat in the sunny conservatory waiting for Santie. I was a born-grubby child, always into something mucky, so Aunty's daily litany for my pristine appearance was wasted breath, because unless collected immediately or kept an eye on I would grow fidgety and wander out to the garden on yet another mud-infested adventure.

With strict injunctions to be good, take care and be back by teatime we set off down the winding lane which led on to the main road, crossed over and waited impatiently at the bus stop. The main road loomed dreadfully in my mind; always called The Road, it was the one place Aunty absolutely forbade me to go alone and dire warnings of its dangers were issued at regular intervals. She preferred us to keep to the relative safety of the winding lanes we walked along every day to school. The fact that huge and potentially dangerous lorries full of stones from several quarries in the area rumbled regularly by squeezing us into the hedge didn't seem to bother her. She only worried about the traffic on The Road.

Bus trips, though exciting, were not very comfortable; the wooden slatted seats pinched our young bottoms cruelly and as my short legs swung clear of the floor I was inclined to slide about quite a bit.

Bumping into each other as the bus flew up and down the hilly, twisting road we giggled into Torquay and, getting off at the seafront, Santie went at once into the Ladies by the Pavilion and emerged sockless, having removed the hated socks in thick white cotton with crocheted tops (doubtless lovingly knitted by my mother) which slid down into the back of your shoes in painful wrinkles.

"Can I take my socks off too?"

"No, you're not old enough; but don't tell Aunty May will you?"

"No."

"Promise?"

I promised.

"Cross your heart and hope to die?"

I crossed and hoped.

Trotting happily along the Promenade, Santie saw some girls from her school coming towards us. They nudged each other, grinning as we approached. I looked from Santie to them, smiling uncertainly and loitering a little behind her, worrying what to do if she went off with them. But instead of stopping to speak to them she suddenly grasped my hand tightly and mothered me along importantly, passing by the girls as though she'd never even seen them.

Was this why we had come to Torquay? Just to pass a few girls without speaking? Classroom politics were unknown to me, as I was a cosseted St Mary's Infant whilst Santie went to the Big Girls' school in Newton.

The seafront photographer appeared so we had a photo taken as a surprise for Aunty May and Uncle Fred. By this time I was getting tired of walking along the seafront and starting to drag on Santie's hand. She was a very sensible child and mindful of my littleness when we were out alone together. Being nearly five years older she mostly found me babyish and tiresome but took me about when her friends weren't available. So we spent a penny, Santie put her socks on again and we got the bus home.

Some time after this jaunt a small altercation took place between Aunty May and Santie, who came flying out of the drawing room just as I passed the door. Seeing me in the hall, she snatched at the back of my collar hissing,

"You told Aunty, you promised you wouldn't; I hate you."

"No I didn't!" squirming away, having no idea what she meant, the exciting trip to Torquay long forgotten.

It turned out that Aunty May, in a rush of sisterly affection had sent the Torquay photograph to Mum and Dad, writing on the back in her large loopy handwriting,

'Happy Easter with love from Santie and Lou, X X X'.

Mum got on the phone.

"Why isn't Santie wearing her socks? What are you thinking about May, letting *my daughter* go out in that bitter wind – you know how it blows off the sea, especially at this time of the year; where's her socks?"

Poor Aunty May, thinking Mum and Dad would be pleased to see their little girls out enjoying the fresh air, hadn't noticed the discrepancy. Feathers ruffled once more, she took Santie to task without mentioning Mum's phone call till much later. Santie was (and still is) very fair and when she learnt the truth instantly came and cuddled me saying how sorry she was and how she knew *really* that I hadn't told as I'd crossed my heart; and she gave me a sweet from her Very Own Ration to make up for it.

You had Ration Books for everything you ate and were 'registered' with only one grocer and butcher per family. Each week was printed in the books and when you paid for your groceries that week was crossed through with a thick indelible pencil. But sweets were different; you had coupons which the lady in the shop cut out from the ration books. They were still dated but if you wanted a big item, or she said something special was coming in, like icing sugar or chocolate, you could save your coupons for that.

Aunty May was scrupulously fair over our sweet rations. She put our five sets of coupons together and when the appropriate weeks came round, got whatever was available. Then, after the supper things were cleared away, Santie and I sat in our usual places at the table facing Uncle Fred and Gramps, who by this time were in their armchairs either side of the big old kitchen range. Aunty would squeeze her considerable bulk into the small space between the sideboard and table and tip out a pile of sweets from the brown paper bag (carefully saved and taken to the sweetshop for the purpose). Then she would smile at us and say,

"Right, now I'm ready to start. Here's a red one for Santie, a red one for Pieface, red one for Uncle Fred, red one for Aunty May and a red one for Grandad." The red ones went round to each pile until they ran out and to make sure no one got more than the others, leftover reds went 'In The Tin'. This exciting ritual then started again with another colour or shape or consistency until the ration was distributed and our little piles of goodies pushed towards us.

"I'll put yours on the sideboard Dad," Aunty had to shout as Gramps was rather deaf. "And yours too, Fred dear, together with mine. You two run away now and don't eat them all at once or you'll be sick."

I'm sure their rations went 'In The Tin' after we'd run off to gorge ourselves because it was a never-empty source of comfort for scraped elbows and knees, squashed little fingers and the ready tears of a six-year-old.

One evening we were doled out a pink squashy toffee-like substance which tasted slightly of toothpowder. We chewed it manfully but it just stretched and became tasteless until finally swallowed in lumps.

"Thaat's bubble gum an' if yer swallow it, it'll swell up in yer insides and y'll die," said my best friend Rose when I told her about the funny pink toffee. After a few anxious days waiting to swell up, Uncle Fred said he was going into Newton tomorrow (Market Day) and would us like to come with 'e? Jumping and hopping about with joy I forgot all about the gum.

Uncle Fred was very old, almost the same age as Gramps and was a widower when he married Aunty May. He was already retired by then, after many years working for the Great Western Railway, ending up as Stationmaster at one of the many little stations on the old Dart Valley Line. Aunty, still at home in South London "looking after poor old Mum" whilst her five younger siblings had married, managed to get away on a holiday to Devon and there met and later married Uncle Fred.

Despite being twice her age they were perfectly content together. Uncle had someone to care for him in his comfortably-off old age and Aunty got a huge house, the prestige she longed for and a leading place in the community.

"May always had ideas above her station," sniffed my mother when she got a postcard from the 'Happy Couple' and Daddy said did she mean Chudleigh or Buckfast? Whenever we went anywhere by train, or had to change at a main station, instead of buying platform tickets Aunty swept us through the barrier crying "Stationmaster's Wife!" to the ticket man. All he could do was nod deferentially and step back smartly as we hurried along in her imposing wake.

Aunty May was a very large woman, beautifully dressed and could be extremely patronising to what she termed 'the tradespeople'. She'd come up in the world at last, was well in with the local Set, those doughty ladies who organised Village events, so why not make the most of it? She got away with it too.

Grandma died at the outbreak of war so Gramps went to live with Aunty. Santie had gone down some months before me and had her nose put out of joint when I arrived. She was Little Shirley Temple personified, all shiny curls and dancing feet, always clean and tidy. You could take her anywhere, she was precociously perfect and the centre of attention.

Then suddenly she had me to share her limelight, a stolid child with grubby knees and a generally scruffy look, who watched everything with intense interest. Poor Santie! Dawdling home from school one fine September afternoon to be confronted with an almost forgotten small sister. I was delighted to see her, she seemed so grown up just like Mummy, who I already missed dreadfully.

To help ease the parting, Mum and Dad had the brilliant idea of sending my favourite toys on before I left London except for Teddy of course, who travelled on the train with me, clutched closely all the way from sooty Paddington. Among the familiar items was a new shiny box and inside a soft, knitted doll with embroidered face and masses of tight, woolly chestnut curls. She had the most beautiful clothes and underwear, all knitted with crocheted string fastenings and a pair of knitted shoes with tiny pearl buttoned loops. It must have taken Mum weeks to make. I called her Shirley and she slept next to Teddy, who slept next to me.

Santie was still at the Village School when I arrived so for a while she took me with her, leaving me at the Babies' door before running off with the other Big Girls. To her surprise, having me tag along gave her new status in her friends' eyes and she started showing me off as if I was a new doll, squashing me into her doll's pram when we played together in the garden.

"You must have the hood up," she'd say, pushing me up and down the paths.

"It hurts my head, I want to get out," starting to sniffle.

For her to seek my company was so wonderful that I would do anything to please her but I was really too big for the pram and Santie knew it. She was quite kind in her way and seeing my obvious unhappiness said,

"All right Lou, if you really hate it, I'll think of something else we can play," and a few weeks later came up with the most exciting game she ever invented.

Chapter Three

"Fred!" Aunty May's voice, pitched upwards to reach the shed at the top of the garden, shouted from the doorway. "The children are all ready. Is Dad going with you?"

"Yes, Mare," came the murmured reply as he appeared from the conservatory, behind her.

"Why does Uncle Fred call you Mare?" I asked. Calling someone a mare was rude, like shouting "you pig!" if you were really angry.

Aunty stopped adjusting my too big beige knitted beret, pushing a hairgrip through the front painfully into my hair to anchor it.

"He never does that, do you Fred?"

"No, Mare 'corse not."

"He said Mare, he said Mare." I wriggled free and hopped round Uncle Fred gleefully.

"He's saying 'My Dear'," said Santie loftily, "that's how *proper* people say it but you don't know anything. Where's Gramps? Is he coming or not?" And off she went, twinkling up the path shouting "Gramps! Gramps!"

Aunty May wasn't coming with us today. She said to Uncle Fred,

"Take the books and get the rations as you're going in, save me a trip. Now Santie dear, you're in charge of the list, don't lose it there's a good girl."

This time we did not cross over The Road; we were going to Newton and that bus stopped our side. Up it rumbled, in we got, me first.

"Marnin' Mr Sherwood, children, Mr Erm." Nodding at Gramps, whose name he'd forgotten, the conductor was helping Uncle lift me on.

"Goin' to get that manooer for her boots and make her grow, are you?"

He chuckled and winked round the bus and the passengers said,

"Aah, love 'er, little pet," as Santie bustled us into a seat, plonking down beside me. Whenever we got on his bus this conductor always commented on my short stature. I worried about manure in my socks so much that one day I asked Santie about it; she laughed and said,

"He's only pulling your leg." As I didn't understand that either she wasn't much help.

Swinging into Newton, jumping down from the uncomfortable, rattly bus into Uncle's held-out arms, we went first to Liptons where we were registered. Santie said importantly,

"I have the list for you," handing it over as Uncle put the ration books on the counter and opened the big bag made of black and red leather squares stitched together, ready to pack in the rations as they appeared. Gramps hated shops and just stood outside, looking through the window at us.

When at last we got to the Market, first passing the penned animals where all the noise was coming from, although holding Santie's hand tightly as she followed closely behind Uncle, I tried unsuccessfully to linger by the warm woolly smell of the sheep. Santie, nose averted, pulled me away. I loved the Market, the brightly coloured stalls, burring voices and laughter but most of all I loved the animals whose baa's, bellows and occasional squeally grunts punctuated the shouts of stall-holders, all yelling at once, trying to outdo each other in their efforts to get us to buy their goods.

"Now," said Uncle Fred after he'd bought what he wanted, mostly a few things for the garden, and met or gossiped briefly with several of his pals. He seemed to know almost everybody there, shoppers and stall-holders alike. "You can have a little present each as you've been such good girls. You first, Santie; what d'you like best?"

Santie had seen a bracelet made of pretty glass beads linked together so she danced over and pointed, smiling at the lady on the stall who wrapped it in a screw of paper. Uncle paid and Santie put her prize carefully into her little handbag.

The three of us moved slowly on from stall to stall, Gramps having gone off on his own business, saying he'd meet us by the Cinema stop for the half-past twelve bus. I was getting tired, dragging my feet, thinking longingly of sitting on the bus going home.

"Look at that, Lou," said Santie, stopping at a toy stall and pointing to a box. It had a coloured picture of two laughing children, a boy holding a disc to his face and a girl with a disc at her ear. There was a piece of string joining the discs to each other.

From the writing on the box I started slowly to spell out each word until Santie said impatiently,

"It's a sort of telephone, we can talk to each other from the end of the garden."

"Would Louise like that then?" said Uncle hopefully. What I really really wanted most of all was a windmill made of stiff shiny yellow paper; there were dozens of them on the stall, whirling round and round in the breeze which blew the familiar animal smells about us. But Santie seemed so keen on the box that I nodded and Uncle handed over the money thankfully, putting the box in the shopping bag.

There was a stall nearby with a counter so high up I couldn't see anyone above it but Uncle stopped and said,

"Aha!" and was handed down a mug of tea. We had 'lemonade', a concoction of flavoured powder, saccharin and water and a small bun with hardly any currants in. Well, at least I got a short rest, squatting down on a thin wooden upturned box thankfully.

"Time's getting on," said Uncle, handing up his mug. "We best go and find yer Grandad and get that bus or we'll be late for our dinners and yer Aunty'll have somethin' to say. Unless you want to go," dropping his voice to a whisper into Santie's ear, "to the Ladies – or can you wait till us gets home?"

We could wait. We found Gramps hovering by the steps up to the Pictures. He looked pleased with himself and when he bent to help me on to the bus there was a rather nice smell, not unlike strong cider apples, about him.

Settled on the bus, Santie got out her present and tried to put the bracelet on but we swung about so jerkily I slid along the seat more than ever, bumping into her so often that, though holding the little chain tight on her wrist, she couldn't do up its clasp at the same time.

"Wait till you gets home or yer'll lose it on the floor," said Uncle, leaning across the bus aisle. Santie sighed and putting the bracelet reluctantly back in her bag, said,

"After dinner, Lou, we'll play with your telephone." She was staring into the distance, head up, blue eyes slightly narrowed; this was her making-up-games look. After a minute she turned a beaming smile on me and the vision of dancing yellow windmills faded as I smiled back at my adored Big Sister.

"What we'll do next," said Santie eagerly, when we were safely home and sitting at the table eating our dinner, "is... "

"What Louise will do next is have a lie-down for half-an-hour," Aunty interrupted. "Look at her, she's dropping over her semolina. You've had a long old morning, haven't you Pieface?"

"Oh Aunty," Santie wailed, her sunny little face turning down, "we're only going to play quietly, honest. She won't have to do anything at all."

Aunty May was adamant.

"Remember Santie, she's not a big girl like you and she must have a lie-down first, then you can play to your heart's content till teatime. Get one of your books now and go and read in the conservatory then *I'll* tell you when it's time to play."

Apart from being good girls, not going on to The Road alone and "not showing me up" when in company, Aunty May had very few rules. Married in her thirties to an elderly husband she had no thought of children until the War thrust us upon her. Happy to get Santie to herself she had plans for making her into what she called "a proper little lady". With dancing and elocution lessons promised and such a willing model, everything was set to make Sant as stuck-up as Aunty could wish.

Then she got me. I learned later in life that Aunty May had not really wanted to take me on as well, mainly because with no experience of bringing up children she thought me too young (and perhaps herself too old) to raise. One lively ten-year-old, with husband and father both well advanced in years, and having to 'Make Do and Mend' as part of her War Effort, was enough; another child, just out of babyhood really and not nearly so winsome as Santie, would be more than she could cope with.

Mum and Dad didn't think it right for me to be in London during the bombing especially as most of the children round about had been evacuated anyway.

"It's not as if she'll be going to strangers," Mum said. "May is my own sister, after all's said and done, and she can't say she hasn't got the room, in that mansion of hers." They eventually persuaded Aunty to let me come down "for a little holiday, to see how she likes it there, with Santie and all; it will be good for her to be with her sister again."

"Mrs Sherwood, we were just saying we don't know how you manage to do so much." This from Aunty's friends, the pillars of society, as we all came out of Church one Sunday morning.

"Your time is so completely taken up with the family and your dear girls, who are such a credit to you."

When we were called 'your little girls' or 'your daughters' Aunty would murmur modestly, then pat at our berets tidily or bend to straighten little coats by jerking their hems. She was very proud of us and well she might be for she brought us up wonderfully. We were loved and protected, chided and guided; Aunty May was HOME and the safest place of all was on her slidy silk-frocked lap in the evening, next to the wireless, which she would tune in with one hand whilst clutching me to her ample bosom with the other.

"We must hear The News, Lou," she'd say as the set glowed orangely and the valves hummed, "see how Our Boys are doing. Be a good girl and sit still for a minute."

Santie never did get those lessons to make her a Real Lady. There was no hope of turning stubborn Pieface into anything other than a happy and contented little girl and as we were treated exactly alike, out the window went singing, dancing and elocution.

"Now," said Santie, as we stood on the path in front of the house, "I'll take the telephone and go upstairs and drop it out of our window to you. Then we can talk to each other with it."

She ran round the drive and in the back door; unless it was an emergency, only certain callers were allowed to use the front door. Our bedroom was in the middle of the large double-fronted late Victorian house, a little room built over the glassed-in vestibule which led from the front door into the dark, narrow hall.

Peering upwards and squinting in the bright light, I waited for Santie to appear and the game to begin. There she was, ducking under the Holland blind drawn down against the afternoon sun (all the window blinds were down that day making the house look asleep). Pushing the window up and leaning out, breathless from rushing up the stairs, she called,

"Here it comes, catch it," and flung one of the discs out. Halfway down the string which joined the two cardboard circles to each other tightened, its knot popped through the dangling cellophane middle and the released disc fell in pieces at my feet.

"Oh, Lou," said Santie, as I stared at the scattered bits, "I'll come down and see if we can mend it."

As I picked it up I heard a muffled snort from above and looking up saw Santie holding her mouth. Then she burst out laughing, slammed down the window and after a few moments appeared once more on the path. "I really am sorry Lou and I didn't mean to laugh but it was so funny and your face! That's one of the shortest games we've ever played. I'll tell Aunty it's all my fault and ask if she'll buy you another one."

"It doesn't matter," I said, "I don't mind," and started laughing too because I knew she wanted me to, knew this was expected of me. I was learning that you laughed when something was said and the speaker grinned or nodded at you. Daddy loved puns, he made them up all the time: once I woke with a bad cold and he said,

"You went to bed my little girl and woke up a little ho(a)rse," chuckling so heartily that I did too although I couldn't understand his merriment.

"All chips and no fish," was another mysterious remark made after I'd fallen over on the gravel path and Dad was washing the 'chips' out of my knees, dipping the cloth in a bowl of stinging Dettol and warm water. I smiled at him through my tears as I knew he was trying to cheer me up. Winsome I might not have been but shrewd I certainly was and could sum people up quite quickly, a characteristic in many a child too often overlooked by adults, sometimes to their cost in later life.

The week after the telephone game that never was, Aunty May and Santie went to Newton together to get the rations, leaving me to "help Uncle and Gramps in the garden." Just before teatime I saw Santie opening the big gate and ran down the drive to meet them. Aunty stooped to give me a kiss, holding her open shopping bag low so I could see inside. Propped up in one corner was a shiny yellow windmill, "for being such a good girl when your new toy broke."

Chapter Four

Rumble, squeak, rumble. Santie appeared round the side of the house pushing her doll's pram. It was a damp overcast afternoon and I was staring up at the woodpile where a blackbird had built her nest. Uncle Fred said there were four eggs and that morning had gently lifted down a greeny-speckly oval to show me whilst the bird 'chuck-chucked' at us from a nearby branch.

He put the egg back, telling me not to disturb the bird anymore but I was inevitably drawn to the spot, so much so that the next day I climbed the woodpile, felt the four little eggs in the soft nest and lifted one out. But alas I was too clumsy and precariously balanced and crushed the egg in my hand. Shaking with fright, I watched the gooey smelly mess and bits of shell spreading over my fingers, trying to rub it off with my hanky. Skulking into the house unseen I washed the guilty evidence away and later 'lost' the mucky hanky at school. I never told a living soul what I had done, keeping my secret until now.

"Loo-eese, *there* you are, want to play?" Santie smiled at me, all the while slowly rolling the pram back and forth.

I eyed it with dislike.

"No. I'm not getting in anymore."

"But this is different; I've thought up a new game." She spoke quickly, to stop me walking off. "All you have to do is kneel down in the pram. Please? Just for me?"

Putty in her hands as ever, I climbed in and crouched down as she clung hard to the wide handle, steadying the pram on the steep driveway. When I was settled she perched herself on the front edge of the pram with the handle in front of her and shouting,

"Hold on tight and away we go!" she lifted her feet clear of the path.

Pram and contents flew down the drive. As we neared the big double gate at the bottom Santie braked by slamming one foot down, making sandal skidmarks in the gravel as the pram slewed round. It was the most thrilling experience I'd ever had and I screamed at the top of my voice. Santie grinned happily round as she stood up, the pram tipped backwards and out I rolled on to the path, giggling helplessly.

"Wanna 'nother go?" Shining-eyed, Santie helped me scramble up yelling,

"YES! OH YES!"

We dragged the pram to the top of the drive, got in and shot down again.

We played the pram game every evening over the next few days. I stopped loitering with my best friend Rose after school, hurrying home instead to get the pram out ready for Santie's return from her school in Newton. Rushing through tea instead of our usual dawdly meal, Aunty May got suspicious.

"Now then, what's the hurry? Don't bolt your food like that, you'll make a rude noise. If I hear even a tiny 'puff-de-loody' there'll be trouble. Gobbling as if you didn't know any better. What are you two up to?"

Santie put her wheedling voice on,

"It's a secret at the moment, Aunty dear, but we'll show you when we're ready, I promise faithfully."

Santie worked on her braking system until we could stop without slewing round but I still fell out each time she stood up. When she decided it was as good as she could get it, Santie invited Aunty May and Uncle Fred to come and see our new game.

"In *front* of the house did you say?"

For a moment Aunty wondered whether she should change her frock. Our nearest neighbour was almost a quarter of a mile away, but being seen dishabille ("in me daisy bill" Aunty called it) was one of her nightmares.

Her most irritating trait, which unfortunately she has passed on to me (to this day still called 'doing an Aunty May') was as follows: each time we went out she would change her dress or coat or shoes, sometimes the entire outfit, at least twice before setting off. Occasionally, when a picnic was planned and Aunty had the sandwiches all ready, slices of National Loaf and fishpaste wrapped in scraps of ancient tissue paper tied round with coloured wool (mine always pink), unable to make up her mind what to wear she'd say,

"Oh blow it, I'm not going and that's that. You can go without me."

By this time it was too late so we'd stay home.

Picnics were fraught with danger for me anyway. If there were cows anywhere near the pretty spot chosen, I was convinced these distant creatures quietly munching grass were really bulls who would come tiptoeing up behind us, breathing down our necks before tossing us all into the air.

"They're *cows* you silly cuckoo," Aunty tutted, spreading out the blue-checked cloth on the grass while I stared nervously at their tummies as only cows wore a glove. Eating sandwiches fearfully, looking over my shoulder all the time, sometimes my terror got so bad I'd start sobbing,

"They're bulls, they'll toss us!" Exasperated, Aunty repacked the basket and we'd trudge home to finish the picnic in the conservatory or garden, where it was safe.

So between Aunty changing her clothes and me frightened that every animal I saw would chase after me, it's a wonder we all went about as much as we did. I was particularly terrified by the pigs that lived near my school; they had their sty at the end of one of the fields. Being so hilly, these fields were as high as the steeply-banked hedges through which the lanes meandered. When the pigs heard us passing far below they chased squealing down the field to throw themselves at the back of their sties. I just knew that one day they'd burst through the hedge and fall on top of me. They never did of course; the farmer wasn't going to lose his valuable pork so you can bet they were securely fenced in.

"Oh, you've got the doll's pram out; I thought it was a new game you were playing," said Aunty as she, Uncle Fred and Gramps stood on the path by the front door.

"It *is* a new game, watch us," said Santie as we got ready. Everything went like clockwork; we whizzed down the drive, stopped at the gate and I pitched out. Aunty didn't like that and was starting to remonstrate when Uncle Fred suddenly spoke first,

"Now Santie," he said, "if you was to stay seated when you stops and hold that pram handle tight, let Lou get out first then her won't tip up. Go on, try it."

Once more we racketed down to the gate and screeched to a halt but this time I stepped safely out. Now it was perfect. Aunty May couldn't get over Santie's ability to make up such an exciting game. They watched us go up and down several times, smiling approval and affection on their little girls.

"When Mummy and Daddy come down next," Aunty said, as we went into the house, "you must show them. Perhaps Daddy will have a go, you never know."

We played the pram game a few more times until one evening pulling it up the slope Santie remarked,

"I wish the drive was a bit longer then we wouldn't have to walk back so often. Let me think," staring at the drive gates.

"Hold the pram a minute, Lou, I've got an idea." Santie ran down and unlatched the double gate, hooking both halves back on their posts, then came back and we took up our positions once more.

Careering down again, faster and faster with no scuffing sandal acting as a brake, we shot through the wide open gate and across the lane. The pram handle hit the hedge opposite, Santie let go and we both tipped out. Nothing in the world could be faster and we raced noisily up and down until I got a stitch and had to stop and get my breath back.

One Saturday afternoon the hangers in the spare room wardrobe rattled ominously and out came our Best Spring Costumes, fine navy blue wool skirts (mine with elasticated top in an attempt to grip it to my non-waist) and bolero jackets. Santie and I were frequently dressed alike although Sant's outfits acquired a few grown-up touches as she grew older. Aunty May made most of our clothes, often carefully unpicking any of her own dresses she considered 'unfashionable' to cut new patterns for us from them.

First she and then Mum, when they reached fourteen years of age, had worked at a local garment manufacturers, beginning by picking up pins and sweeping floors, being taught 'fancy' sewing and graduating to doing the most exquisite and intricate beadwork, all by hand, stitching this on to a thin backing. It was then appliquéd with tiny stitches on to the chiffons, nets and organza evening gowns sold in the big London stores and worn by fashionably smart and well-heeled women during the Twenties. Needless to say Mum and Aunty earned a pittance for all their beautiful painstaking work, the posh shops getting the profit from their labours.

Aunty continued to sew all her life but Mum, after she married and had us, took up knitting as it was easier on her rather weak eyesight, not helped by years of sweating over the tiny glittering beads. She became so proficient a knitter that after the War she worked for one of the big knitting pattern companies as a 'checker', working from written instructions, altering and amending as necessary. We all got a kick out of seeing the actual jumper or cardigan (then called a sports coat) she'd knitted worn and photographed on a model.

"That shoulder decrease is perfect now but didn't it take some working out?" Mum would say, squinting sideways at the picture through the Wool Shop window when her latest creation appeared 'in print'.

One winter she knitted twelve teddy bears, stuffing them with kapok and knitting little green and red waistcoats as well, for a special Twelve Days of Christmas pattern book feature.

Mum had a tight deadline on that job, working day and night to complete it so Santie helped to embroider their faces and each one had a different expression. The pattern people were delighted and paid Mum a bonus; her 'Circle of Teddies' appeared on the magazine cover and we were very proud of her.

No wonder Santie and I were so well turned out, wearing Aunty's renovated smart silks and crepe de chines for 'best' while Mum, knitting needles ferociously clacking in far-off London, sent beautiful jumpers and berets, gloves and socks winging down to us at frequent intervals.

I got Santie's left-offs which, with identical outfits, meant I wore most things twice. If I disliked a particular frock it would be worn in the gloomy knowledge I'd soon have another just like it.

One year we got pink gingham frocks which we adored. Aunty must have been a bit short on material as these didn't have the usual enormous hems 'for growing into' but were in fact quite skimpy, with little puffed sleeves. Santie's version had inverted pleats in the skirt front and instead of ties stitched each side (fastening together at the back) hers had a separate belt in the same material with a tiny ivory buckle. This time I could hardly wait for the hand-me-down but as we wore the dresses practically all that summer they both finished up in pieces in the 'Make Do and Mend' bag and the coveted ivory buckle was saved to reappear more than once on Santie's frocks.

So there we were that Saturday afternoon, scrubbed and shining in our matching costumes and Mum-knitted white jumpers, waiting with Aunty on Newton Station for the London train bearing Mum and Dad. This time they were to stay for a week, entailing more luggage than usual, so Aunty May had "ordered the car" as she put it, meaning asked the local garage owner to fetch us.

"The children have got a lovely new game to show you," Aunty said beaming at Mum, as we bowled along The Road.

"After you've unpacked and had a cuppa we'll go and watch them playing, shall we?" It was lovely to see Mum and Dad again and Santie and I were excited because we had a new audience to show off to.

Waiting quietly on the driveway, Santie having latched the gates back ready, after what seemed like an age they all trooped out, smiling indulgently at us.

"Are you ready then?" Santie looked towards Aunty.

"Yes, yes; off you go love, show Mummy what you showed Uncle and me," said Aunty, making shooing movements at us.

Away we rumbled, speeding through the gate and disappearing from their view into the lane, shrieking as we tipped over. Mum and Aunty got to the gate just as we picked ourselves up.

They stared at us in horror, their mouths big round O's, until Daddy joined them, saying,

"Put that pram in the shed and go inside at once," in a Very Tight voice. He had gone very pale and was starting to wheeze, his shoulders heaving as an asthma attack took hold.

We ran off, frightened and confused, with Mum shouting,

"And go straight to your room, I'll deal with you later," as she and Aunty helped Dad into the house.

"What have we done?" I asked Santie as we sat side by side on her bed. I started to cry and she put her arm round me, rocking from side to side.

"Don't cry, Lou, it'll be all right. You see, Daddy's been ill again and Mum says he suffers all the time." She stroked my hair soothingly but her voice was quiet and strained, not like my chirpy Santie at all.

"Will we get into trouble?"

"I don't know," she replied unhappily.

My sobs got fewer and finally gave way to huge yawns. We got ready for bed and lay listening to Mum and Aunty going at each other, their angry voices rising and falling to the clattered accompaniment of supper being got ready.

"There's nothing more to be said, May. They could have been killed rushing into the road like that. Supposing one of those great lorries had come round the corner? They wouldn't have stood a chance."

"I've told you a thousand times, I didn't know they had the gate open. When we watched them playing they just went down the drive. I never dreamt they were going into the lane, how could I?"

"You need eyes in the back of your head, you know what kids get up to as well as I do. I leave my children in your charge and *this* is what's going on behind my back. When he saw them in the road I thought Jim would have a fit. Hark at him up there, coughing his heart out; I must go and see if he wants anything."

Mum was right, Santie and I could hear Dad coughing continuously in the spare room.

Aunty kept repeating,

"I swear to God I never knew," in a broken voice but just then Mum came out into the hall saying,

"Oh damn – look, we left the door open." Then she said more gently,

"All right, May, I know, it's not your fault, it's nobody's fault; it's this bloody War getting us all down. We'll say no more about it but try and have a nice little holiday with the girls, all of us together, if Jim's up to it."

We fell asleep, unaware that Mum had looked in, bringing us hot milk and a biscuit. No matter how cross she got Mum's policy throughout her life was "never let the sun set on a quarrel". But this time she tiptoed away bearing her peace offering back without disturbing us.

"Seems a shame to wake them, poor little things," she said pouring the milk into the saucepan of water Aunty had put on the stove for their evening cocoa. "My, this is a treat, eh? Better than made with just water!" And they sat chatting far into the night, talking over old times and new, friends once more.

We were unusually quiet at the table the next morning, eating porridge, as Mum and Aunty made us promise never to ride in the pram again. We could "play nicely" with our dolls in it, like proper children not harum-scarums, but this was too tame for us after the heady excitement of before. So the pram got left in the shed and was eventually given to the Children's Home.

Daddy felt better after a day's rest, well enough to come to Torquay with us "for a bit of a blow". He didn't scold, just shook his head reprovingly at Santie before holding out loving hands for us to grasp and walk proudly either side of him, as we all crossed over The Road to wait for the bus.

Chapter Five

Br-r-r-ring. The doorbell echoed through the house. Aunty May, on the lookout behind the drawing room curtains, hurried to open the front door.

"Oh it's you, Doctor Black." Affecting surprise, as though this was an unexpected social call instead of a telephoned-for visit, Aunty still managed the deferential tone reserved for 'the professional classes'. Like the Bishop, the Vicar at St. Mary's, or indeed anyone from any of the churches regardless of denomination, Dr Black was allowed in the front door so we knew he was Important.

"I'm afraid Louise seems worse today. Please go up, Doctor, the children are in my room."

We had The Mumps. Santie caught it first from school and was now getting better but not before, in the usual hand-me-down fashion, she had passed it to me.

"And how is dear Sandra today?" boomed the doctor, coming along the landing and beaming at us round Aunty May's bedroom door. He was under the mistaken impression that Santie's name was Alexandra and always called her Sandra but because he was important Aunty wouldn't dream of contradicting him. In fact Santie's nickname was for being born on Christmas Day.

Dear Sandra and Little Louise were sitting in soft velvety pink chairs either side of the window in Aunty's lovely big pink bedroom. We each wore one of Uncle Fred's white silk scarves tied round our heads and swollen necks; Santie was trying to read me a story but I could only grizzle in painful misery.

We loved sitting in Aunty's room, looking out over the sloping roof of the bay-windowed drawing room, where Ginger got stuck once and Uncle had to get her down with the laundry basket on the end of a broom handle, held out of the window enticingly. Although our own room's central window gave the best view across the fields to the soft hills the other side of The Road, where tractors crawled like tiny red or blue beetles clinging to the impossibly steep slopes, from Aunty's window you could see further down the lane, where it curved and dipped away to the left before rising up again to meet The Road.

But even Aunty May's beautiful pink bedroom held a terror for me in the shape of a dark and frightening picture, a depiction of Christ's head wearing the Crown of Thorns. Wherever you were in the room, the eyes followed you; but sometimes, if you turned suddenly and stared at the dim browny-green face, the eyes were *closed*. I tried not to look at the picture in its dark gloomy frame, hanging over Aunty's pink eiderdown; this satin delight was invitingly soft, scrolled stitching making fat little cushions of each intricate pattern, just asking to be bounced joyfully on.

I didn't say anything about my fears as sitting by Aunty's window was a Special Treat; but Aunty, quickly noting the direction of the frequent glances over my shoulder, would say,

"What is it, Pieface? A spider? No? Well, something's worrying you. Let's see now... aha! I know," and she would turn the picture's face to the wall and everything would be All Right again.

Another of Aunty's looming frights, The Shrine, lurked on the landing in the dark corner where the passageways to the front and back of the house converged. At the top of the stairs was the huge window which looked out over the back; to the top end of Mrs A's paddock next door and high over the hedges at the bottom of our garden dividing us from Mr Miller's fields, where the Railway runs beyond through deep cuttings to Totnes.

I loved this window and stopped to look out every time I went upstairs, even if busting 'to go.' Sometimes I'd watch Uncle Fred and Gramps working amongst the vegetables and fruit when I was supposed to be lying down resting, then Aunty would call up,

"Well, if you're up anyway Lou you might as well come down." I never could discover how she knew, believing myself invisible behind the glass.

You turned sharply right here, passing Aunty's room on the left then into our tiny room, just the width of the landing, at the end. There was a huge grandfather clock outside our door which went TCHING! TCHING! all day and night, unless people stayed, then Uncle Fred had to stop the clock because they complained it kept them awake. But we found it difficult to sleep without that old clock's pendulum clonking back and forth and its floor-shaking TCHING! TCHING! silenced. It was unnatural. We missed the way it would start wheezing and whirring itself up a minute or so before its magnificent voice shouted through the house.

The lavatory and bathroom were to the side of the house with Gramps' room beyond at the very end and going along the back landing meant passing the Shrine but at least it didn't watch you, like that picture did.

"There's nothing to be afraid of, you silly onion," Aunty said, as I drew shudderingly to the farthest edge of the passage on my way to the bathroom before bedtime. "It just shows you Jesus is protecting all of us."

Not me it didn't. All I saw was a small dark and dimly lit table with a white lace cloth, upon which stood a silver Crucifix with two silver candlesticks either side, their flickering candles, lighted at night, making ghostly shadows of the Cross on the wall behind. There were a couple of china figures with their hands folded and heads bent and I would run quickly past with my own head averted.

It wasn't so bad at Christmas, when the silver objects were removed and several small candles lit up a Nativity Scene, with a dear little crib and a tiny Baby Jesus in it inside the stable, the roof painted to look like thatch. The figures weren't quite so frightening now as they had a few china animals for company and Mary kneeling by the crib in a lovely blue dress.

Aunty May's bedroom became our safe haven at night too, when planes droned overhead and Aunty woke us up to be brought, sleepily stumbling on the darkened landing, to her room.

"Is it one of Ours?" The same question was asked every time as we settled by the window with Uncle Fred and Gramps before Aunty drew the heavy blackout curtains back, eyes straining at the black sky, trying to see the plane.

"Yes, it's one of ours, we're all safe." Always that reassuring answer. But if I caught even the tiniest hesitation before Aunty replied, I knew it was one of Theirs.

I was constantly told "There's a War On" but thought this was something to do with London from which Santie and I were sent away. There was somewhere called Germany where Our Enemies lived.

I had heard about Hitler – he was an Enemy so obviously lived in Germany, though he'd visited Torquay as once we passed a shop near the front with broken glass and rubble where the window had been. Propped up on a large piece of brown cardboard was a chalked message saying HITLER PASSED THIS WAY. I wondered why Aunty hadn't mentioned him coming, or got our best coats out for us to see him.

Hitler had been on the bus too. There was a drawing of him sitting behind two ladies, one of whom had a hat just like Aunty's. They were chatting away and Hitler was leaning forward with one ear cocked at them. CARELESS TALK COSTS LIVES was written under the picture. Whenever I saw this poster I turned round to see if he was sitting on our bus behind Santie and me but he never did.

COUGHS AND SNEEZES SPREAD DISEASES – TRAP THE GERMANS BY USING YOUR HANDKERCHIEF, *my* reading of another poster in the bus. As Dr Black took care of our coughs and sneezes I suppose he trapped the Germans too.

I couldn't ask him though because I was wary of Dr Black. He was a good and kindly man; he made The Mumps go away so I could go back to school, which I loved. But he once was the totally innocent cause of me getting into serious trouble with Aunty May.

"'Ere, Lou," said my best friend Rose during morning playtime, "do you like ice-cream?"

"Ice-cream? What's it look like?"

"En't you never 'ad ice-cream?" She turned round unbelieving eyes on me, rubbing her tummy and saying, "Coo, it's luvvly, you'd luvv it honest."

"Oh I expect I have then Rose," I said airily, "in London probably. Why?"

"Well, I hear'd they got ice-cream in Fuller's Dairy over The Road. Tuppence each. Us c'd go and get some arter school, shall us? If yer got tuppence?"

Rose's elder sister appeared at the gate as we left school that afternoon to go on an errand together which Rose had forgotten about. I watched them go up the hill to the Village and stood hesitating, wondering what to do. Having made our plans it never occurred to me just to go home and wait for another day.

So I followed them slowly, fingering the four ha'pennies in the leather purse I wore on a long strap across my frock. Instead of going into the Village, if you turned left by the cottages where Rose lived and went down Forge Lane you came out on The Road, right opposite to the Dairy. At the top of the hill I turned left.

For the very first time I was alone on The Road. How noisy it was and so vast it seemed to stretch away in each direction for ever. And such a long way across! Surely it was never this wide when Santie was with me, or Aunty May? Hesitating nervously on the kerb I stared at Fuller's Dairy; shall I, shan't I? But I wanted that ice-cream very badly and eventually greed became stronger than fear. So, as soon as a really wide gap appeared in the traffic, I crossed over The Road, all by myself, my mind full of ice-cream and what it might taste like.

"Allo," said a large lady in a white apron who was leaning on the counter as I entered the shop. "What d'you want then? En't you Rose's little friend from Lund'n?"

"Yes. I want some ice-cream, please." I held up my four ha'pennies, standing on tiptoe as the counter was very high.

She lifted the hinged flap, opened the counter front and came through grinning,

"Ice-cream is it? Let's see what's in y'ere," pointing to a huge metal box at the side of the shop.

As its lid was opened a lot of steam wafted out, like when Aunty took the cover off a pan on the stove and said "mind out, Pieface, this is hot!"

But standing close behind the white apron I began to feel very cold.

Diving inside this monster, she handed me a little white round brick, icy cold, with a piece of paper the exact size stuck to its edge. I said "thank you" politely, gave her my money and left. She was still grinning as the shop bell ding'd me out.

Waiting to cross The Road, I shifted the ice-cream from hand to hand, regretting having come so far on my own just for this cold white stone. Now I must walk all that way back, up steep old Forge Lane and down Constitution Hill to the school with a further good mile still before I got home. With Santie or Rose chattering alongside I dawdled to my heart's content but alone and tired, my adventurous spirit rapidly died. Besides, the ice-cream was beginning to squash in my hand and a blob fell over my fingers and on my sandal. Sucking my fingers and licking round the delicious papery cover till all the ice-cream was gone, I wandered home.

"Where HAVE you been, you NAUGHTY girl!"

Aunty darted into the lane shouting as I came in sight of the house, anger giving her voice a definite London cast. Santie was hanging over the gate, having alerted Aunty to the wanderer's return. "Why are you so late? I've been worried sick, Uncle's been down almost to the school twice looking for you."

"Coming home from school." In the self-centred way of childhood, I could not comprehend that anything I did when I was out on my own affected those at home. Alarmed by this unexpectedly hostile reception I decided to modify the truth.

She ran me into the house, Santie dancing ahead to get out of the way. There was going to be a row and she didn't want to miss any of it. She flew upstairs to squat in our secret hiding place, under the big gate-legged table on the landing above. If you leaned close to the banisters and providing the door into the hall was left ajar, you could hear what was going on down in the back room quite easily.

"Coming home from school, eh? And what time do you call this?" Aunty pointed at the cuckoo clock which amazingly said quarter to five, nearly two hours since I'd left school.

"It doesn't take two hours to walk home, not even the way you dawdle along with that friend of yours."

Aunty didn't approve of Rose because she was from the Village.

"She's not really Our Class," she insisted. Class was what you were in at school and Rose *was* in my class, so what did Aunty mean? She wanted me to play only with the nicely-behaved daughters of her friends, those too-polite, too-tidy children, content to sit and read or play with dolls. They never climbed on the hedges or puddle-hopped, or squashed tarmac bubbles with their sandals in the lane on hot days, like Rose and me. Margaret, Audrey and Christine were like the dolls they played with so earnestly, pretty but lifeless.

Mind you, Aunty was always nice to Rose in her patronising way but Rose was all too aware she didn't meet Aunty's stringent standards.

"Yer Anty doan' like me," she'd say shaking her head in refusal whenever I asked her in to tea.

"Yes she does, that's not true."

But my earnest denials became more doubtful as time passed and now I was almost seven and a half and sadly knew Rose was right.

"Now, Louise, what have you been up to all this time? No good I'll be bound, you and that Rose."

"Just coming home from school." Clammy with fear, staring at my stained sandal, unable to look Aunty May in the face, knowing I was 'for it' this time.

"All right then, *I'll* tell you where you've been, since you won't. You've been over The Road, on your *own*, after everything I've said, *and* telling your poor old Aunty lies."

My head jerked up and I stared at her in disbelief. She *knew*, had known all along. Did God point His finger out of the sky at me to show Aunty where I was? He did sometimes if you weren't good; there was a picture just like that on the wall in Sunday School and people were cowering on the ground to get away from the pointing hand.

What could I do? I'd been Found Out yet still stuck doggedly to my story.

"No I haven't, I've been coming home from school – the long way round," I added by way of amendment.

"Don't lie Louise, I'm not daft. Doctor Black saw you coming out of the dairy of all places! He was getting into his car to do his rounds, but took the trouble to go back in the house and telephone me. He didn't think you should be there on your own and wondered if I knew. I was so ashamed when he told me. What were you doing in Fuller's anyway? You know we're not registered there."

So, Doctor Black had split on me and then gone blabbing to Aunty May, eh? Not God after all, unless Doctor Black had glanced up as he got into his car and seen the finger pointing at my head.

"I went to get some ice-cream."

I was starting to cry.

"Ice-cream? What ice-cream? Where is it then? Melted all down you, by the look of you!"

"I et it," snivelling, still looking down at my stained sandals.

"Et it? You et it? This is how we speak now, is it? Mixing with that Rose. I suppose she put you up to it, did she? I notice you were by yourself though. Why didn't Rose go with you? Even that would have been better than you wandering about on The Road on your own." Aunty was beginning to calm down.

"Well, you're home now and with all that ice-cream I'm sure you won't want plain old shepherd's pie for supper, will you? Not that you deserve anything at all, telling stories like that; I don't like little girls who tell lies. Now go to the bathroom and have a good all-over wash. I'll come up in five minutes to see if you're clean."

Snotty-nosed and tear-stained, I went slowly upstairs, too miserable to heed Santie's "psst!" from under the table; so unhappy I even forgot to be frightened of the Shrine.

Gramps had made me a small wooden box with green baize nailed to the top as I was too short to reach right into the basin and standing on this I ran the water in; swishing my flannel around in it, I began half-heartedly to scrub the sticky stains off my face and hands. After a while I heard Aunty May come up the stairs, go into our little room and, after a minute or two, came along the landing and into the bathroom. She sat down heavily on the too-small stool, leaning back against the blue walls which were covered all over in cut-out wallpaper seagulls, which dipped and danced along and above the dado rail. The knobbly-glassed window had blue and white check curtains, the left-over material of which had gone to lengthen Santie's blue dungarees two years before.

"Come here and let me see that neck; why, you could grow potatoes in the muck behind your ears!" With these words Aunty drew me to her and I turned and buried my face in her large, comforting 'apples', crying bitterly. Aunty stroked my head.

"Don't cry anymore, Louise; look, you're making my blouse all wet. But I hope you've learnt your lesson. You must never never tell lies, not to me, not to anybody. It makes us all unhappy and there are enough things in this world to be unhappy about without my old Pieface upsetting me. Try to be a good girl and not wander off on your own like that. Promise?"

I nodded vehement promises and really meant to be good as gold. Aunty May sighed, shaking her head; she knew that quite soon another enticing scheme would present itself and I'd forget everything else and be off again, roaming the countryside, after my own rainbow.

"Good. Now let's get you properly washed and a nice clean dress on; but you will have to say sorry to Santie and Uncle Fred and Gramps – they would have liked some ice-cream too you know. You should have told me about it first and then Santie could have gone with you – not that I approve of any of you going in that dairy though," she said, whisking the flannel round my ears and neck, soaping arms and legs and feet, where even my toes through the sandal pattern had received the odd blob of ice-cream.

"I've got your green flowered frock ready to put on." She eyed me, head slightly on one side, waiting for my usual wail of,

"Oh no, Aunty, not the green one"; but not this time. I was her Pieface again and would wear it for ever if she asked me to.

"Will you come down with me, please Aunty, please?"

"Of course I will, we'll say sorry and then have supper. But Louise, you mustn't play out this evening, nor tomorrow. You can sit in the conservatory and read before bedtime, but no running about in the garden. Do you understand?"

I understood. I was being punished, but oh so gently. The fright I had got in being found out was enough punishment to last me a very long time.

We went downstairs at last, me clutching Aunty's hand tightly as she opened the door to the back room with its red polished kitchen range. This was where we ate and played and listened to the wireless and wrote letters to Mum and Dad at the big old table. They were all there, Gramps washing his hands in the large kitchen beyond, Uncle in his armchair by the conservatory window, Santie already in her seat at the table.

"Louise wants to say something to you," said Aunty, urging me forward. "Go on, you're keeping us all waiting."

Head lowered in shame, I stared at the carpet, its glowing squares and oblongs of gold and yellow, each pattern outlined in brilliant red and black 'teeth' , like the top of the turret room in the castle that Rapunzel let down her long hair from so that the king's son could climb up and rescue her. I would push my clockwork engine up and down these carpet 'lines', moving slowly across the thick woolly surface till my knees ached or Aunty said,

"Don't crawl about under our feet, there's a love. Why don't you get your railway lines out and play with your train properly? Uncle will slot them together and wind up the engine if you ask him nicely."

But I preferred my carpet rails to the cold metal circle the tin lines joined into. Anyway, the carriages always came uncoupled or the engine wouldn't take the curve where the rail had got bent and fell off, on its side, wheels whirring uselessly. I was in total command of the entire GWR on the carpet – driver, fireman, stoker and guard all rolled into one. The Railway was in my blood; Uncle Fred's tales were bearing fruit.

"I'm sorry," I mumbled.

"Eh? What's the child been up to now?" said Gramps, coming from the kitchen.

"She's sorry she kept you waiting, Dad," yelled Aunty May; "come and sit down, that pie'll be stone cold soon if we don't eat it."

"Oh good, I'm starving. Get in, Lou and we can start." Santie was grinning and moving out for me to get to my chair in the corner. Uncle leaned forward, ponderously knocked out his pipe on the side of the range, picked up the plates that were warming on the hearth and put them on the table then sat down facing Santie. Gramps shuffled into his chair next to him. Aunty May came at last from the kitchen, cloth'd hands clamped each side of the dish, calling,

"Mind out! This is *hot*! Is the mat ready?" like she always did, plonking the pie down on the big oval table mat.

My horrible adventure was over, I was home and safe and would never leave again – until next time.

That night I was just drifting off to sleep when Santie leaned over and tugged at my eiderdown.

"What was it like?" she asked.

"What? What like?" I said sleepily.

"The ice-cream of course, silly."

I'd already forgotten its taste; it had been washed away with the flannel and my tears.

"Don't know. Night-night, sleep tight, see you in the morning". And, having said that, our nightly prayer, I went to sleep.

Chapter Six

"Hurry up, Louise, you'll be late. What are you doing? Edward's here, he's waiting. Come on, dear."

Let him wait. I was busy. Last night after supper, Aunty got out an old shoebox full of photographs.

"I must sort these out and stick them in the album. But I never get time these days, oh well, never mind. Let's see what we've got. Oh look, here's one of Santie, ah-h, just like a little fairy, up on your points. Can you remember this being taken? No, you look too young. What's Daddy written on the back: 'Santie, aged 3 years'. I don't expect Louise has even seen this one – why, it was before you were born, Sweetheart."

With this, she slapped a sepia picture down on top of the rough paper I was making pictures on with coloured pencils. Pencils were safer in the evenings, when the table was laid ready for breakfast the next morning and you pushed the plates to one side to make a space on the cloth. Using paints, which involved much twirling of brushes in an old fishpaste jar filled with water, was only allowed when nobody wanted the table for hours and, providing it was spread with many layers of the *Daily Mirror* and I wore an all-enveloping apron, kneeling up on my chair to paint a lovely picture for Aunty May was most enjoyable. And when even making coloured swirls into the water with my brush began to pall, I would start reading the latest news on the sheets of paper laid any old how under my drawing book. In this way I quickly developed the very useful facility of reading upside down or sideways as easily as the right way round.

Any occupation of a splashy nature could be hazardous for me and those around anyway as from very early childhood I had developed a nervous twitch, made worse by anxiety or excitement. On a bad day my arms would spasm too and away would go the cup or plate and contents, to cries of,

"Oopsy! Never mind, love; we'll soon clean that up."

These little blips were ignored by nearly everyone and I was unaware of being 'different' – until I dropped something or was suddenly swooped on and crooned over by sympathetic older girls.

"It's the War that's caused it, all that dreadful bombing, poor little mite," tutted Aunty's friends as they patted my head. But a pal of Uncle Fred's who happened to call round, seeing me digging in the garden with my seaside spade remarked that my 'clumsiness' was all the fault of being cack-handed. But Santie and Mum were left-handed too and they didn't spill their tea or 'need a little rest' before going out to play.

One afternoon Santie, chatting with her friend Isabel near the railway bridge by the school, caught an older boy copying me twitching as I came through the gate. She darted after him, swung him round and hit out hard, knocking him against the railings, whereupon he started blubbing. Then, after putting her arms protectively round me for a moment, she took hold of my hand, saying,

"Come along dear, we're going home now. Give Isabel your other hand and we'll give you a swing. One, two, three and U-U-P-P you go!"

I couldn't believe Santie was being so nice, especially as she was with Isabel; usually she tried to pretend I wasn't there when her friends were. Not one to miss an opportunity for being fussed over, I 'whee-e-e-d' happily up and down between them. When we parted from Isabel and were walking up the lane, I remembered the boy, whom I knew vaguely from Sunday School, wondering what he'd done. So I asked Santie why she went for him.

"He was being rude, that's all; don't let's talk about it anymore." As she spoke she jutted her chin up, turning her face away from me but not before I noticed the two pinky spots on her cheeks. This was Santie's way of saying, "private, keep out." I stayed silent, occasionally glancing up at her as we walked along and although she smiled back each time, her clouded face showed that something had really upset her, although I seemed to be in the clear for a change.

As it turned out, Aunty May, Santie and me saw the boy's mother in the Village the following Saturday, on our way to get stamps to post our letters to Mum and Dad. She was talking on a corner with some cronies and started to complain to them as we walked past, saying about his father being away in the War and having to be mother and father to the lot of them, then all of a sudden like he'd been set upon in the playground by one of 'they Vackees'. Aunty's mouth tightened, she glanced back, paused and drew herself up, saying haughtily and loudly to no one in particular,

"If a *boy* of mine had been smacked by a *little girl*, I shouldn't want any of my friends to know what he was doing to deserve it. Come along, children, we've a lot to do this afternoon." And she swept us on up the High Street.

"Louise! Hurry up for goodness sake; Edward will go without you in a minute!"

Let him go then, I don't care. I was standing in front of the dressing table, which was squashed cornerwise next to the window. I had lined up its two side mirrors with the middle one in the vain hope all three together would reflect me from head to toe, instead of only head and shoulders as usual, and was trying to copy the photo of 'Santie, aged 3 years'. She was dressed in a frock with a top just like a vest but the skirt was lovely, sticking out all round like a saucer. She had her arms above her head, hands joined and wore a circle of pom-pom flowers on her curls and a dear little necklace to match.

Even in plain school clothes I managed the arms and hands pose, head tilted prettily, to my satisfaction. The difficult bit was trying to balance on my tippy-toes like Santie was doing. Her feet were curved right in and she wore shoes like my doll

Shirley had on, with ribbons crossed over her ankles. Try as I would, I kept tottering to one side, thumping one foot down and clutching Santie's bed cover so as not to knock against the dressing table and make the glass dishes on it rattle together. As I was hopping up and down at the same time, trying to see my legs and pointed toes in all three mirrors at once, Aunty must have heard the thumps and bumps as she stood in the hall because she suddenly yelled,

"LOO-EEZ! COME DOWN *AT ONCE*. Edward is going NOW!"

I really couldn't care less if he goes, so there – then I remembered the pigs and flew down the stairs straight into Aunty May, who had one foot on the bottom stair and was coming up to,

"Hook you out of it, once and for all."

Running off down the hall, through the back room and out the kitchen door shouting,

"Wait for me! I'm coming," I chased round the house to catch up with Edward as he crunched determinedly down the front drive to the gates.

"*I* don't want to be late even if you do," he said crossly, looking round at me as I panted along by his side. "I shan't call for you if you keep me waiting. I've got Arithmetic first this morning so we must hurry."

He was a studious boy, a year or two older than me. When Santie went on to the girls' school in Newton, Edward often walked me to the main school building where my class was, before going up Constitution Hill to the tin-roofed Village Hall where some of the older children had their lessons. On rainy days the teachers had to shout because the constant drumming on the roof almost drowned out their voices.

The Infants came out earlier than the Big Ones so I didn't bother waiting for him in the afternoons but meandered home in my private dream-world, trying to absorb everything I saw, walking so slowly that Edward sometimes overtook me. Then he would tell me what he'd learnt that day, most of it going right over my head.

"As Father is away at the War, I must look after Mummy and take care of things," he said importantly. Endlessly patient both with me and his younger sister, he was far too serious ("just like a little old man that boy is sometimes," Aunty used to say, "still he's steady and dependable and very good with Louise"). I found him rather dull. He wouldn't do anything adventurous, just walked straight along the lane to school and back home again with no diversions on the way. If I stopped to pick a flower or watch a bird, Edward said,

"Oh come *on*, Louise, do try to keep up, you're lagging behind again."

One frosty morning I suggested we 'cow-stepped', a winter game Santie taught me when she first took me to school. It was really exciting but Edward was shocked at the suggestion.

"We mustn't do that," he said, "it's trespassing and besides, it'll make us late for school."

Edward took his responsibilities seriously and was as much a worrier as me in his own way, with my fears of being tossed or eating poisoned berries and dying, and I was glad of his company going passed the pigs. He pooh-poohed my terrors, saying they couldn't get at me and anyway, if they fell that far they'd kill themselves. I still wasn't entirely convinced and glanced nervously up as we heard them squealing and thudding against the pens.

As long as I didn't dawdle or dart from one side of the lane to the other but walked fairly briskly by his side, Edward helpfully pointed things out he thought would interest me. He knew the names of every flower, bird, little furry animal and even which plane was flying overhead. But really, if I couldn't go to school with Santie I would rather be on my own. At least she had some sparkle in her; I even missed her hanging on to the back of my collar, which I hated, to stop me running off.

"Stop wriggling, Lou; if you promise not to run away I'll let go and I've got an idea. Let's go in the gate of the field next to Honeypots and I'll show you a new game. Come on."

The gate was slippery with glittering white frost, making climbing over hazardous, so Santie unhitched it, closing it carefully after I danced through. We were to walk along the field inside the hedge and out through another gate about 100 yards further along the lane. Edward would think that a complete waste of time, but to Santie and me it was tremendous fun.

During the night the frost had frozen the muddy ground hard and where the cows had trodden the day before their heavy feet made deep holes with a skim of ice on top. The game was to walk carefully along the crusty mud ridges around the holes. Santie was very good at this, almost running from ridge to ridge, calling,

"Come on, Lou! It's easy, just copy me. Try and go a bit quicker."

I tried. The ridges were narrow and my legs very short. I teetered on a rim, lost my balance and one foot went down, through the thin ice and splap into freezing water.

"Santie, I'm stuck!" I yelled, wobbling about with one foot on the ridge and the other down the muddy cow-print. "Come back, get me out!" I was cross that I couldn't cow-step like Santie, couldn't copy her deft movements; the fact I was too little to play the game occurred to neither of us. Louise was being clumsy again and couldn't do it properly.

"Oh honestly, Lou, I told you to be careful." An exasperated Santie weaved back along the ridges; grasping my middle and heaving me out, the water made a sucking plop as my leg came up covered in red sticky mud to the knee. "Just look at your sock! You'll have to ask Miss Digby to dry it when you change your shoes." (The Babies put slippers on when we got to school, leaving shoes tidily on the bench under our numbered coat-pegs).

"I didn't mean to fall in, Sant, honestly. Poo! don't it smell horrible!"

Safely rescued, Santie's familiar snort of laughter set me off. My balancing act so short-lived I was still by the first gate, we giggled out again on to the lane, me squelching along at Santie's side until we reached school. To my surprise she came inside with me, grasping my hand, straight up to Miss Digby, who was coming to shepherd her arriving flock into the cloakroom, supervising the coat-unbuttoning and pixie hood-undoing.

"Good morning, Miss Digby." Her clear high voice rang out and the children and a few grown-ups that were about looked round curiously. "I'm afraid Louise has got all muddy, she stepped into a muddy puddle and her sock is all wet."

Miss Digby, who I loved best after Teddy, Aunty May and Santie, said,

"Oh, poor Louise. Here my pet, let's have that old sock and I'll give it a little wash. But you'll have a cold leg this morning, till it's dry, won't you? Put your slippers on and we'll dry your shoe at the same time. Thank you, Santie, you're a good girl to bring her straight to me."

I looked quickly at Santie who was smiling her social smile but I caught the tiny movement of her mouth towards me and for the first time we became conspirators, both knowing the 'accident' was our own silly faults and we would never let on to anyone, ever.

All morning I could see my long sock steaming woollily on the black shiny guard round the huge fire and my shoe, cleaned of its sticky redness, drying close to the fender.

"Reckons 'er 'opped to school this marning," said Eileen to her friend Lily, staring at my sockless leg after Assembly. Lily was a *real* evacuee, living with Eileen and her mum in the Village where she had miserably arrived one cold afternoon with a suitcase, gas-mask in a cardboard box with string handles and label tied to her coat.

52

"Nah," said Lily, "spect 'er sister lugged 'er. That's wot I 'ates wiv the country, Eileen, it's muddy all the time. Ain't got no nice pavements to play on nor nuffin'. On'y fields. I 'ates fields, I do reelly."

My cow-stepping improved with a bit of practice on dry days when the holes were shallower, but I never achieved the ease with which Santie balanced so deftly. When Edward refused my offer to show him how to do it I was quite relieved and could keep the game secret between Santie and me. Anyway, Edward hardly ever played out after school; he busied in his patch of garden or in the paddock, looking after his chickens and rabbits.

As if he hadn't enough to do, Edward came round regularly to see our rabbits, handling them gently, making sure they were healthy and properly fed. Everybody kept small livestock in their gardens, feeding them scraps saved from dinner.

"Don't play with your food, Louise; are you going to eat that cabbage or shall I give it to your bunny? *He'll* eat it up and no mistake. Make him big and strong."

One Friday after school, as I passed through the kitchen on my way to play in the garden, Aunty said,

"Don't bother about Bunny today, Pieface; Uncle and Gramps are cleaning the hutches out. Don't you go round there disturbing them now."

I felt guilty at being reminded about my rabbit; I frequently forgot to feed him or clean him out. I liked him very much, he was soft and pretty though his feet scratched when you cuddled him. I couldn't believe he was real; rabbits ran about in fields or hopped across the lane in front of you. In my eyes he was the same as the furry toy rabbits Aunty made; each Easter Sunday and at Christmas a new one would be sitting waiting on the chest of drawers when I woke up.

Teddy and my dolls were real. Teddy listened to my troubles and comforted me when I hurt. We talked together as I fed them imaginary cakes and cups of tea from pretend cups.

Santie couldn't understand my apparent uncaring attitude, didn't listen when I tried to explain, so I kept my confusion to myself. Tired of waiting for me to share the chores she took on both rabbits, grumbling about it not being fair whenever I remembered Bunny and dashed round to his hutch to find her there already, busy with clean straw and fresh water, offering the juicy greens and pieces of carrot they loved.

Santie must have a lot of homework to do if Uncle Fred was cleaning out the rabbits. I wandered round the corner and stared in the empty hutches. After a few minutes Santie joined me.

"Uncle's done them," I said. "Have you got a lot of homework or do you want to play hide-and-seek?"

"Not much; anyway it's Friday so I needn't bother right at this very moment. All right, I'll play, but just for a little while. You hide, I'll count."

I rushed happily away as she started counting loudly,

"ONE, TWO, THREE... "

Squashing myself behind the wood-horse, where Gramps cut tree branches up into logs or stakes for the garden, I crouched down, holding my breath as Santie gabbled on then shouted,

"NINETY-NINE, A HUNDRED! I'm coming!"

Peeking out through the wooden sides, I saw her hesitate on the path, looking away from me. Staring at the grooves made on the crossed legs of the 'horse' as the saw slipped sometimes, I remembered when Mum and Dad were down one wintry weekend and Daddy came to help Uncle and Gramps cut some logs. There was a lot of laughter and a soft whistling sound coming from the woodpile and, being the nosiest child on earth, I went to see what was happening.

Daddy was sitting on the stone seat nearby, the handle of the saw between his knees; his hands were gently curving the saw and the high-pitched sounds came as he bent it back and forth.

"If I had a bow I could do 'Bells Across the Meadow'," Daddy said, smiling at me and giving the saw back to Uncle Fred.

54

"You can have mine," pointing at the ribbon clipped on a slide in my hair and Daddy laughed heartily; getting up he ruffled my bow and said,

"Not that one, darling, it's not big enough. Now I must go in but I'll tell Mummy about your kind offer."

Daddy was a self-taught musical genius, almost a One Man Band. He learnt to read music in the Salvation Army when a small child and mastered the tenor horn, playing in their band. From this beginning he moved to the strings, playing ukulele and banjo, the latter with his younger brother, a good semi-professional pianist.

When a young man he took up the trumpet and French horn and joined the local district Silver Band, still playing tenor horn but usefully able to double-up for missing members – especially when War came and they got called up. It was a very good Silver Band and at one time played under the conductorship of the then very young Harry Mortimer (later knighted and still revered by aficionados, including myself, today).

One of my very earliest memories of Daddy is one sunny afternoon, sitting on Mummy's lap on the end of a row in front of a park bandstand, Santie on an iron slatted seat next to us.

"There's Daddy, look, in his uniform," Mum whispered, pointing at a figure who looked exactly like all the others on the bandstand and could have been any of them.

After a while, growing fidgety on Mum's slippery lap, I slid off and, the music now skipping joyfully along, that's what I did, up and down the aisle by Mum's seat. The people sitting nearby grinned and chuckled at this three-year-old 'dancing' in the sunlight. When the music stopped and Mum scooped me up, they clapped the Band warmly but smiled at *me*.

Through Dad patiently tuning my musical ear as we listened to concerts on the wireless, I began to hear as he did and to sing in tune. That I should learn to play a musical instrument never entered my head, though once piano lessons were mentioned; but that would cost money which we didn't have, so nothing came of it. Not that it bothered me: I just sang on, learnt to hit the exact note Dad wanted as, tuning fork ping'd to start me off, he 'pointed' me up and down the musical scale. Dad's reward came later, the day I rushed joyfully home with the news I'd got a place in the London Schools' Choir for their very next concert in Westminster, and could be in line for a solo spot.

Mum, laying the table for dinner, suddenly remembered when I danced in the park long ago.

"What surprised me, Jim," Mum paused, pointing a handful of cutlery at me, "was how perfectly in time with the music she was for such a little thing, didn't miss a step."

"I'd have been surprised if she hadn't been, wouldn't I Tuppence?" Daddy was grinning proudly. "You heard me practising enough to know all the tunes and counter-points, taking it all in." Then he said seriously, "Your *voice* is your instrument now Louise, and you must 'play' it the very best you can. Whatever happens, don't ever give up. Promise me?" Daddy sighed, for by then the crippling asthma had fatally taken hold and his band days, along with his shining tenor horn, were long gone.

"Your Dad can get a tune out of anything," Gramps said quite admiringly, which was high praise coming from him. Short in stature and temper, used to ruling the roost at home, living in Aunty's house had clipped Grandad's wings.

"Bloody lodger, that's what I've come down to," he grumbled. "Might just as well be in the Workhouse."

He wasn't too fond of Santie and me either, particularly if we were larking about, letting off steam. But he could use his increasing deafness to his advantage, ignoring us at will then complaining we left him out of things.

"Should have been called Grumps instead of Gramps," Santie muttered to me one day when he told Aunty we'd been annoying him on purpose.

"I heard that! I heard you, you little madam!" he shouted as we ran off laughing.

Grandad didn't seem to mind my company as much as he did Santie's and I would hover round him sometimes in the garden when I hadn't any mischief to get up to. Aunty May always sent me to fetch him in for meals on his 'deaf days'.

"I'd rather you go, Pieface, he won't grumble at you like he does Santie," Aunty said when I complained. I learnt, all by myself, to circle the garden so he could see me first, waving to attract his attention, instead of going and yelling 'GRAMPS!' in his ear, like Santie did. I'd mouth 'dinner', pointing to the house and he'd nod as I ran back.

"I CAN *SEE* YOU!" shouted Santie, bringing me out of my reverie, making me jump. But she was still looking the other way, in fact hadn't moved off the path.

"How did you know where I was?" Amazed, I squeezed out from the horse – I was getting too fat to hide there much more; I never used to get so scratched on the bushes before.

"Oh, were you there? I'm just fed up with playing, that's all." And Santie walked away round the corner into the house, leaving me stupefied. Santie had *cheated*. We never played hide-and-seek again.

On Saturday morning as the smell of cooking began wafting through the house, Aunty said,

"We're having a nice stew today, as the weather's turned a bit cold; it'll warm us all up," Aunty was briskly peeling spuds at the sink. "Do you want to help with the carrots? You can eat a piece if you do."

I didn't, but I loved raw carrot so, with a tea towel wrapped round me I knelt up on the kitchen chair and with a blunted knife scraped away busily.

Santie came in near to dinner-time. She'd been down to the church with Isabel, something being planned involving the older children.

"What's for dinner, Aunty? Smells nice."

"Stew. Louise did the carrots for me. Wash your hands, you too Pieface, and sit down ready." Then, shouting out the door, "DAD! FRED! DINNER!"

Steaming bowls in front of us, I dipped in my spoon. Santie let out a cry of horror, jumping up and pushing her bowl away,

"It's RABBIT! It's RABBIT! Oh Aunty, how COULD you?"

She ran crying into the hall, thudding up the stairs, slamming into our bedroom. Aunty just stared at the ceiling, then looked down at me.

"You'll eat it, won't you? At least eat the vegetables and you can leave the rest. You don't have to copy everything Santie does; she's not always right." But Aunty looked unhappy, Santie was sobbing and I didn't want my dinner anymore. If Santie wasn't going to eat it there must be something wrong.

"I knew there'd be trouble letting them make pets of them. Yes, you did warn me, Fred; I know, it's my fault. I don't even fancy it myself now, what a waste. Still, you men are tucking in, that's a blessing. I better go up to Santie, poor little thing, it's really upset me."

Aunty got ponderously up and opened the hall door, then paused and said to me,

"There's some nice stewed apple for Afters, Pieface, or do you want a bit of bread and BeTox instead? Uncle Fred will get it for you, won't you dear?" And she went down the hall towards the stairs.

Chapter Seven

When I paid attention to what he was saying, some of Edward's nuggets of learning began to lodge in my brain and I started to ask questions. Then later I'd sift the bits I could understand and tell Rose what I knew, though I was very muddly about some facts, particularly anything scientific.

Edward talked of planets and comets, said the world was a ball and twirled round all the time. I didn't believe him. I thought of the shiny coloured map covering half the classroom wall that Miss Digby pinned little flags on where 'Our Al-eyes' were; I supposed her Al-eyes were cousins or something.

"No, it's not round, it's flat and has got flags on. Look, the horses are in the field, let's get some stuff for them," running off down the lane to pull out cleaver from the hedge. Cleaver was funny; if you threw it at someone it stuck to their clothes. Grown-ups got angry if it stuck on them.

"Don't do that, child, it's dirty," they'd tut, picking the grass off, attempting to throw it away. It clung tenaciously to their gloves and no matter how much they shook their hands the cleaver wouldn't budge, so in the end they asked you crossly to pull it off and put it back in the hedge where you found it. Well, you got told off but it was worth the scolding as a grown-up losing dignity was screamingly funny to Santie and me.

I stood on the bars of the gate, dangling the cleaver at the two horses and they ambled over to see if we had any apples or a bit of turnip for them. Sometimes they ate our grassy offering, mostly gently snuffed their broad noses at us to be stroked. Bobs and Charley, farm horses with long manes and immense white 'feathered' feet, giants who pulled the combine through the fields and trundled loaded carts along the lanes.

"Which is which, do you know, Edward?"

"That's Bobs with the white star; that's Charley. Or is it the other way round? I must go in now and see to my rabbits and feed the pony. Bye, I'll call for you tomorrow – don't keep me waiting though."

Edward turned in at his gate and set off up the winding path past his vegetables and huge Shirley poppies, all of which he grew from seeds.

"You're lucky with Edward, the boy's got green fingers," Aunty May said to Mrs A when she brought round a bunch of his flowers for Aunty's birthday. I stared at his hands for ages afterwards but they remained the same grubby pink as mine. Aunty had said Uncle Fred was colour-blind; was I too?

"Am I colour-blind, Aunty?"

"What frock have you got on?"

"The blue one with white polka dots."

"Sandals?"

"Brown."

"Well, if you know that why d'you ask? Run away and play; try and keep that blue frock with white polka dots *clean* for a change."

Waving to Edward, I walked on up the lane, scuffing my shoes on the tarmac, humming tunelessly. Looking up, I saw Santie come round the corner towards me and ran to meet her, waving and shouting.

"Do you *have* to shout and tear about like that in the lane?" she said, the aura of girls' school still hanging about her, making her feel important and bossy. Aunty May was delighted with Santie's increasing hauteur but when she considered my sister was getting a bit above herself, particularly in her attitude to me, Aunty told her to try and leave the school on the bus when she got off. So completely incomprehensible was this request that I didn't even bother to ask anyone to explain it to me.

"Oy-oy! Here comes Miss High School," Gramps regularly said loudly through the open window that overlooked the drive, as Santie came along. I thought this very funny, hopping about

chanting "Miss High School!   Miss High School!" until,
realising it made Santie very angry, Auntie told me to stop
being so silly.   Santie's face would go red, she'd toss her head
and slam through the room to hang her coat, hat and gas-mask
case on the hallstand.

"Now look what you've done, Dad, upsetting her like that.
It's a silly thing to call her anyway; you should be glad she's at
the good school instead of making fun of her."   Aunty May
spoke sharply and, fearing Santie would dart upstairs and shut
herself away, went into the hall saying,

"Come on, Santie dear, you know Gramps doesn't mean it
and Louise is waiting to start tea; aren't you hungry? Your
tea's poured out.   Come and wash your hands and sit down,
there's a dear."

Santie, who hardly ever bore a grudge for long, sat at the
table with me, eating bread and dripping with a scrape of
BeTox on top, chattering as usual; but she wouldn't speak
directly to Gramps for ages.   When my bedtime came Santie
often came with me and had her wash, then went down in her
dressing gown for another hour, seven o'clock being too early
for a Big School girl to go to bed.

I did the rounds, stretching to kiss bent-down cheeks.

"Night-night Aunty, night-night Uncle, night-night
Gramps."

"Santie going up too?" suddenly asked Gramps.

"She's coming down in a minute, just for a little while
longer, Dad. Why?" Aunty May called out from the kitchen,
where she was washing up the supper things. Gramps nodded
and went back to reading the paper.

When Santie came to bed at last she nudged me awake then
said,

"Are you awake? Look what Gramps gave me," opening
her palm to reveal a shiny sixpence, a whole SIXPENCE, such
immense wealth making me gaze at Santie, open-mouthed.

"Well, I had to say goodnight to him too, couldn't really leave him out, and he sort of mumbled 'here you are, gal – nighty night'."

Putting the sixpence in one of the glass dishes on the dressing table, she bent over the saucer with the night-light in, its dim flickerings making a small comforting glow, then half-turned an enquiring face to me.

"Said your prayers? OK to blow the light out?" Pouff! Santie clambered into bed; although the room was pitch dark, I knew she was grinning as she said,

"You know, Lou, I don't mind Gramps making me angry if he does this. D'you think if he does it again I might get enough for us both to go to the Pictures on Saturday? Night-night, sleep tight, see you in the morning."

I snuggled back down under my comforting eiderdown, its padded grey softness a reminder of last Christmas when we went up to be with Mum and Dad in London, for there I had seen barrage balloons, cigar-shaped and squashy-looking with a fat quilted tail, tethered on long wires, waving gently high up in the sky. I thought they were stitched out of little bits left over from grey eiderdowns; like Aunty made our clothes from pieces in her ragbag because everybody had to 'Make Do and Mend', so the eiderdown factory made balloons too.

I pointed at the barrage balloons, asking what they were for and Daddy said they were to stop the Enemy Planes. How? Did they bump into them?

"No, darling," said Daddy, "it stops the Enemy flying in low at night to avoid the radar. The planes get caught up in the wires and the man on the big gun shoots them down."

Daddy always spoke quietly, never ever raised his voice, and the unfamiliar, noisy surroundings of a London bus made it hard for me to catch every word, let alone try and make sense of it.

How could planes get caught up in the wireless if they had to avoid the radio? What was the radio? There was a man on

Aunty's wireless sometimes who introduced dance bands by saying,

"This broadcast is brought to you by the magic of radio," so only the Enemy had to avoid it because Aunty always listened.

"It's nice to hear American music for a change, even if it isn't very clear," she'd smile, turning the knob to "bring it in a bit, see if we can't stop it crackling; hark at it, sounds like 'Frying Tonight!'"

"Tell you what," said Daddy, "when we get home if you look out of the side window in the front room you'll be able to see our own balloons, over in the park."

"Our very own? Can I have one to play with?"

He laughed, said no, they were far too big and heavy to play with and lots of people were needed to hold them till the wires were secure. They only looked tiny because they were high up, like aeroplanes. But aeroplanes *were* tiny, weren't they? Just little silver dots flying overhead?

"No, they're huge," then curiously, "Louise, don't you know things look smaller the further away you are?" It would be a very long time before I could grasp the principles of perspective.

I craned upwards, trying to see the balloons from the bus window but we sat downstairs so I saw only grey trodden grass, the tethering wires and a lot of people in dark uniforms. I clutched Teddy tightly because he hated the noisy, dreary London streets too, with their strange sooty smell. I liked Paddington though; like Newton, its smell was the familiar, friendly one of steam trains whose shrieking engine whistles echoed into the high, distant roof. You were all right so long as you clung on to Mummy or Santie's hand though you still got bumped with heavy bags as you were pulled through the sea of rushing legs.

Mum and Dad lived on the ground floor of a yellow-bricked house in a rather genteel, leafy suburb which meant crossing the whole of London to get there, changing buses, laden with cases and boxes; to arrive at the tall dark house, the last one in the row of identical terraced houses, at the bottom of a long hilly street, thoroughly tired out and grizzly.

"Here we are, home at last," Daddy said, opening the front door. "Let's get in quick and get the fire going. Mummy left the Valor on in the sitting room to take the chill off. Mummy'll get you unpacked and I'll go and put the kettle on."

He coughed away and went round drawing all the heavy curtains before putting on the lights, which only seemed to add to our gloom. The sitting room smelt of paraffin and furniture polish and the black iron stove made a lovely pattern on the ceiling of the darkened room, like a huge daisy. You could move a little tongue on the top of it and the 'petals' went smaller. I thought it was magic.

Stretched out in front of it on a small piece of carpet on the lino was a big black cat, with green eyes and a tiny stump for a tail.

"This is Blackie," said Mum, "say 'hallo' to him, he's very friendly. I expect he'll let you play with him later on."

The cat stood up, arching his back and waved his stump in greeting, purring and sleek. He made up a little for the slightly forlorn atmosphere of the half-forgotten house.

"Why hasn't he got a tail?"

"He's been ill but he's better now. Daddy found him with a great big bump on his tail. The PDSA had to cut it to get rid of the bump as it was poisoned and Blackie would have died. He's lucky Daddy found him in time."

Posters urging you to save petrol, to walk short journeys instead of catching the bus (although it ran anyway, whether you got on it or not), meant that most people used bikes to get about. Dad was a 'real' cyclist from his youth, belonging to a club; he was a great advocate of the outdoor life, so cycling to work in The City every day was second nature. Besides, he couldn't bear being closed in and had difficulty breathing if shut up too long in a bus or tram. He preferred to be out in the open although pedalling in London's smoky air did nothing for his chronic asthma.

Dad worked a five-and-a-half day week so on Saturdays he was home by dinner-time, except that once in a while, instead of coming straight home to tend his vegetables in the small patch of London clay known as 'the garden', he and one or two friends would cycle round the rubble-strewn bomb sites rescuing stray or injured cats and kittens. They'd probably run off during an air-raid and got left behind when their owners were bombed out. If the cats seemed fairly healthy – hundreds of city workers shared their dinner-time sandwiches with them – they let well alone; but the poor old things were taken home and nursed back to health.

Once on the mend, colleagues and neighbours were cajoled into giving 'a lonely little cat' a home; Dad said it gave you something else to think about besides the War as a cat purring by your side was such a happy sound. He was very persuasive and many cats found new families through him.

Daddy pedalled back after the round-up, ding-dinging 'I'm home!' on his bell and Mum would hear the familiar miaow-miaow coming from his saddle bag.

"Oh no, Jim, not another one! Give it here, let's have a look," and she'd bathe its wounds and feed it up on precious milk and bits of meat from their meagre rations. If the cat was in a bad way Mum and Dad went to the PDSA for advice. Often the animal was too far gone and would have to be put to sleep and Dad would say,

"Well love, I suppose it's all for the best, put him out of his misery. Cecil and I will have another look round soon and hope for better luck next time."

There was something else in the flat, even odder than the tail-less cat: the back room contained the most enormous table I had ever seen. It almost filled the room it was so big and high; hard as iron, it clanged when you kicked it and even with three cushions on the tallest chair I hardly reached my plate when I clambered up. You could have sat ten people round that table easily.

"What a big table! Who else lives in here?" swinging my legs into a vast emptiness.

"Nobody else, silly, only us; there are other people upstairs, don't you remember? So don't start wandering about, stay down here. You haven't got the run of *this* house like you do at your Aunty's. If you want to 'go' it's through the back door, on the left; Santie, you show her, unless you've forgotten as well. And Santie, while you're at it, try to cheer up for goodness sake, this is supposed to be a holiday not a funeral."

Mum was getting annoyed, irritated that we weren't excited to be 'home', hadn't rushed in joyfully at once but instead stood glumly, holding hands.

"It's time you two came home, sulking and acting like strangers in your Own Home. The sooner this War ends the better..." her voice grumbled on.

"Let 'em settle in, Grace, don't start laying down the law before they've hardly got their coats off. Give them a bit of time." Daddy the Peacemaker, smoothing her down, reasoning,

"It's a damn long journey for anyone, let alone children, on their own in the guard's van. You'll see, something nice and hot inside them now then off to bed and they'll be right as rain in the morning."

Santie's misery communicated itself to me but at least I had Teddy for comfort. I didn't like the tall houses and samey streets all round us and longed for the fields and muddy Devon lanes. Aunty May tried everything to stop us going and a lot of cross phone calls ensued; but Mum was adamant and home we went, the day before Christmas Eve.

"Bloody miserable Christmas we'll have, Ginger, won't we?" I heard Aunty saying to the cat as she packed our cases. "Why the hell Grace and Jim wouldn't come here for the holiday I don't know. But no, she must have it her way."

Aunty May didn't want us going all that way on our own, even though Santie was extremely sensible most of the time and could be trusted not to do anything silly. But Aunty couldn't leave Uncle Fred, who was getting increasingly forgetful, or Gramps, to their own devices, especially at Christmas.

"God knows what they'll get up to without me watching them all the time."

Savoury smells were wafting into the room through the open door which led into the kitchen, its heavy black-out curtain twitched to one side. Next to this door was a large window.

But the only view you got when you looked through was into the glass-roofed kitchen. The strict Wartime regulations about not showing lights at night meant that Dad, like his neighbours, had covered the roof glass in black paint. So even if there was anything to see, you couldn't, it was so dimly lit. So there we were, all glassed in but, unlike in Aunty's conservatory, you couldn't see out. These windows going nowhere were very mystifying.

Tucked behind the kitchen, never getting any direct sunlight, the back room was always cool and rather dark. There were no proper windows, just a small square fanlight set high up, next to the cavernous ceiling. Dad had fixed a pulley to it, from which a thin looped rope hung, the ends twisted round a metal knob screwed low on the wall. Making flourishes like a magician he'd pull one side of the loop, shout 'Ta-dA-A!', and open or close the window at will. I never tired of this trick.

With Mum clattering about in the kitchen and the room warming up because Dad brought the Valor stove in to supplement the skimpy coal-rationed fire, I began to feel more cheerful. And when a large steaming dish appeared on the table even Santie took notice. Mum was clever with food; she could conjure up a tasty dinner out of a few potatoes, couple of carrots, a sliver of meat and gravy browning. She scored over Aunty, whose cooking left a lot to be desired. It was edible, but dull.

Mum and Aunty May were very much alike, though Mum denied it strenuously, both in looks and temperament, the latter inherited from Gramps. Large, stout women, whose short tempers were quick to rise and feelings easily hurt, always jealous of somebody, usually one another. Only in cooking skills did they differ; Mum's food was a treat, tasty and well-cooked. It was almost worth coming to London for.

"Now children, wire in," she said, spooning vegetables and gravy into steeply rimmed plates, "this'll do you good, put some colour in your cheeks. Louise, don't stick your nose in the plate like that, it's not poison. She still smells everything, Jim, d'you see? Just like Pip. I'd have thought May would've put a stop to that. Sit up, duck, eat properly."

"What is it?" sniffing appreciatively. "What's Pip?"

"Soldier's Pie. Don't tell me you've forgotten your Uncle Pip! Or Uncle Arthur I should say. Dad called him Pipsqueak because he was the youngest. He's in the RAF now, there's a picture of him on the sideboard in his uniform, looking very handsome I must say."

Mum's anger had passed; the sight of us tucking in with enthusiasm softened her. Wrapped up in herself, worrying over Dad's worsening health, postwoman by day and up half the night making Christmas things for our stockings, she hadn't given any thought to coping with our actual presence. She had a misty picture of the four of us together with Santie and me looking and behaving impeccably, something like the photograph in the *Express* of 'The Two Princesses At Home'; having us there, dependent on her for everything, wasn't going to be easy for any of us.

"Now, Louise, I'm going to tell you the secret of this big table," said Daddy, as we scraped spoons round our plates so as not to miss any carrot that might be lurking at the bottom. "When you've finished and had your wash – you too Santie, early night, you're tired out – this table will be transformed, with a wave of Mummy's magic blankets, into a B-E-D! There! How's that for a little bit of London magic, eh?"

Chapter Eight

I was dreaming. Lost in the midst of a huge crowd of people running and shouting. The noise was appalling; an immense thumping as they bumped against me, then a horrible tearing, splintering sound, like hundreds of trees all falling down at once. Terrified and sobbing, hemmed in by hurrying legs so I couldn't run away, I made a supreme effort to escape and woke up. Shaking with relief, I became aware that the noise hadn't stopped with the nightmare; it was all about me still.

Turning over I could just make out Santie, sitting bolt upright in our cosy bed under Mum's magic table.

"What's happening? Is it a thunderstorm?"

"I don't think so, Lou, it sounds different. Probably an air-raid."

No, it couldn't be; air-raids were quiet things. Sometimes at night, when the planes droned darkly overhead and Aunty got everyone up, including Ginger, to sit together in her room or under the stairs, the muffled 'boom-b'm-b'm' of guns could be heard down towards Torquay. If this constant loud banging was anything to go by, London air raids certainly were different.

What a lot I had to tell Rose; I could boast all day at school – a London raid and we were right in it! Even Lily would be impressed. Having no sense of danger, I wriggled about excitedly.

"There are people in the hall all talking at once and someone went out the front door just now," Santie put a restraining hand on my arm. "Sh-h a minute, I'm trying to hear what's going on. Oh, that's Mum speaking now; I think she's coming to see if we're all right."

Mum came clomp clomping down the two stairs that led to the back room, where we were tucked up in the Morrison Indoor Shelter.

"Mr Morrison thought some of us would like a shelter indoors instead of in the garden and some people haven't got any gardens to put them in anyway. Now he's the Home Secretary he has to keep everybody safe in their homes. That's what HOME Secretary means. So Mummy and I said yes, please Mr Morrison, we'll have one. And no, Louise," Daddy twinkled, seeing me opening my mouth to interrupt, "he didn't bring it round himself. He's too busy helping Mr Churchill win the War."

"Aunty May says everybody in London's got an air-raid shelter under their gardens like a cave with steps going down into it, with tables and chairs, everything, in them." Santie was so well-informed and knew so much that I gazed at her proudly.

"Andersons they are, Next Door's got one, full of water when it rains and cold as charity," sniffed Mum. "Anyway your Dad couldn't sleep underground now, could he, not with his cough. No, this is much better and I've got a nice big table to work at too. Your Aunty doesn't know the half of it; you'll have a tale to tell, won't you, when she hears we've got an indoor shelter and you slept in it."

Dad couldn't use the Morrison either as he had to sleep sitting up, propped on a wooden backrest and many pillows. So his head knocked against the underside of the table-top, unless he kept it bent down with his chin on his chest, making him cough more than ever. Mum's bulk made it difficult for her to get in and out but anyway she preferred being with Dad in the huge front room which led off the hall.

"If it's our turn, we'll go together," she said. Their bed did get blown across the room once during a daylight raid, as the legs folded up under it; luckily they were at work when it happened.

Santie disliked being shut in under the table but I didn't mind. It was an adventure, something else to regale Rose with. Anyway, you didn't lie right on the floor but in a sort of metal box with low sides and a mattress in the bottom. Thin steel frames made of wire mesh squares hooked on to the bolt-heads along all four sides, enclosing you in a cage. This was supposed to protect you from flying glass or bomb damage. You unhooked them in the daytime: propped against the wall, the frames rattled loudly every time you opened the door.

The first night we got in bed and Mum started hooking the frames round, Santie got out again quickly, refusing to go back if we were to be locked in. Supposing one of us wanted to go to the lavatory?

"I'll leave the door ajar so if you want to just call out and I'll come and let you out."

Santie was beside herself, shivering with fear, crying,

"I'm not getting in, I'm not! I'm NOT! Don't make me, please Mummy."

Mum was surprisingly sympathetic, nodding and saying,

"I know you hate being shut in, Santie dear, just like your Dad you are, but we must keep both of you safe. Let me have a think: What if I just put the top and bottom on and leave the sides open? That'll keep the blankets tucked in one end at least. Will you get in if I do that?"

Reluctantly Santie nodded, slowly climbing in, putting her icy feet into the bit I'd warmed up. She was shaking with cold and after Mum had gone we hugged each other close, snivelling together, finally falling asleep from sheer exhaustion. Santie was so strong, hardly ever cried, so when she did it upset me dreadfully.

The side frames were never used again during our stay. Years later, after the War had ended and the Morrison taken away for scrap, they still remained in the back yard, lying against the wall, rusting reminders of a dark Wartime Christmas.

"I bet that little lot has woken the children up," Mum was speaking over her shoulder as she came into the room, making the frames rattle in the draught from the door. "Yes, I knew it, Santie's awake. Everything's all right, duck; nothing to worry about. No, don't get up, there's a good girl, you'll wake Louise."

"She's awake already, Mum. Have we been hit? Where's Dad? I'm getting up anyway." Santie's voice was quiet and serious, talking to Mum like a grown-up.

"No, we're all safe, thank God, and Blackie's in his box here in the kitchen. Not much disturbs this cat, he's been through it all before, haven't you old boy? Get up if you want to then Santie, and I'll make some cocoa. Yes, Louise, you too; can't leave you out now you're awake, can we?" Mum was being so cheerful and soothing even I was suspicious. "It will take half the night to boil the kettle though as I'll have to put it on the Valor; mustn't chance the gas, not in a raid."

Banging the kettle down on the warm Valor stove in the corner of the room so it blotted out the daisy pattern on the ceiling, rattling cups and saucers on to the table top, she continued,

"Daddy's gone out to see what's what; can't stand being in when there's a raid. He puts his tin hat on and walks round the houses, checking for incendiaries. 'I'm doing my bit for the War, Mummy', he says. He'll be back soon to tell you all about it. Might as well have a biscuit while we're at it; won't get any more rest tonight."

It was quarter to three in the morning. I had never been up so late in my life. The thumps and crashes got fainter and, after a short eerie silence in which the sound of voices calling to each other carried quite clearly across the gardens, the wailing siren shrieked out the All-Clear.

As if she'd been holding her breath all that time, Mum puffed out,

72

"Phew! That's over, thank the Lord; Dad'll be back in a minute and if he brings in another cat, I'll brain him. Come on kettle, boil for goodness sake."

There was a scuffing of feet at the back door and the handle rattled, followed by a soft knocking. Mum ran to open it, crying,

"Ooh, sorry Jim, forgot to take the bolts off," and a very dusty Daddy came through, rubbing his hands.

Shining his torch on Mum's feet, he said in a deep gruff voice,

"PUT THAT LIGHT OUT!" Then he spotted Santie and me sitting at the table and pretended to be amazed, falling back against Mum and shading his eyes, stunned by the sight. But he was grinning all the time.

"Well, well, this is a nice surprise. Good afternoon, girls, I trust you slept well; how are you today? My word, it's a bit parky out there," blowing on his fingers, "is there any cocoa on the go, Grace? Let me get my breath back," as we clamoured round him, "and I'll tell you what's happening."

A mysterious change came over Dad when he was out Fire Watching for which no explanation was ever offered; Santie and I saw it a couple of times that Christmas. Each time he returned after his stint instead of the usual wheezing, bow-shouldered Daddy we knew and loved, a brisk upright man hurried in, bright eyed and ready to sit half the night telling us stories, making puns.

His crippling asthma, ageing him before his time, briefly left him whenever he got called out, along with the other good people from their homes, at the first note of the siren's hated up-and-down wail. Clapping his tin hat on, Dad would almost *run* out of the house, this man who, on a bad day, went up steps one at a time, pausing for breath on each one.

But only a very little while after his safe return Dad's painful wheezing bark and the rather pleasant smell of his herbal cigarettes 'for medicinal purposes' were once more the background to our lives.

"The old church this end of Baxter's copped it. Nothing but the front wall left standing but funnily enough, the cross on the top is still there." Baxter Road was the next but one to ours; we'd had a close shave this time. "They'll have to pull it down though as there's nothing behind it."

"Anyone hurt? Have a biscuit, Jim, you look done in. Do you want a plate?"

"No thanks, love, I've got one of my own, full of teeth just waiting for that biscuit." This was Daddy's joke for he had worn false teeth, 'my plate' he called it, since his youth. "Nobody hurt, no houses damaged. Just the church, a direct hit. You'd think that Jerry was aiming for it; perhaps he got lost, couldn't read his map in the dark and mistook our church for Buckingham Palace, eh?" He and Mum laughed heartily together but Santie and I just stared, uncertain. Where was Grumbly Mum and Quiet Dad? We didn't recognise this cheerful couple smiling at each other as though we weren't there.

"Made an awful mess of the road though. They're trying to clear it now, but the main's blown; you'll have to cook on the Valor again as it might be days before they can mend it. You better start now, you know how long the roast took last time!"

"Ah-hah! That's where you're wrong, see." Mum was tapping his arm playfully. "We're invited round the Harrises again today, had you forgotten?"

"Today? I don't even know what day or night it is, ducks. Well in that case, we'd better all get a bit of shut-eye or we'll be good for nothing later on. You two, shoo!" Then singing, 'Under the table you must go, ee-I, ee-I, ee-I, oh!' as we scrambled in, putting on an affected voice he said, "Good night children, everywhere," just like Uncle Mac did at the end of *Children's Hour* on the wireless.

We heard Mum and Dad whispering as they went along the hall. Another bad raid over and they'd come through safely, still in one piece. The same pattern was repeated night after night over most of England: sleep for an hour or two, siren goes and you get up till the All-Clear. Then back to bed, doze off before siren screams through your dreams and you get up again.

Come morning, totally exhausted, getting by on skimpy rations, you went to work; Dad on his bike to The City, Mum in her postwoman's uniform to her sorting office to collect the heavy bag of letters for her 'walk'. Everyone wanted letters; good news or bad, Mum felt she was keeping families in touch with each other.

"Come on Louise, try not to dawdle, there's a good girl or we'll never get there. Tell you what, why don't you run ahead for a while, warm yourself up, put some colour in your cheeks."

But I felt sullen and headachy, too tired to run anywhere, walking along a pavement with just houses lining the road either side held no interest either. I missed the hedges and fields and there were no horses to talk to. Going round the Harrises seemed such a long way too. Santie took my hand, giving it a little squeeze, asking,

"Did you bring your new colouring book with you and pencils?"

I nodded.

"The last time we came this way Father Christmas had left presents in our stockings, hadn't he?"

Realising she was trying to cheer me up I warmed to her, grateful to have something other than this tedious walk to think about. So I began to chatter on, my mind running in all directions, wiping glittery hoar frost off people's gates on to new woolly gloves as we passed.

Early on Christmas morning we had woken up in pitch darkness, scrambling to the bottom of the bed to see if Santa had been. Yes! Two fat bulgy stockings lay there, waiting to be opened. Dragging them up, feeling all around the outside, from rag dolly on the top with long yellow wool plaits to shiny apple and almond in the toe.

It was wonderful: chalks, coloured pencils, drawing books, a spotted dog made of tin that you wound up, knitting set, jigsaw, dear little flower brooch, everything. And sweets! Lots and lots of sweets. Mum and Dad must have saved up their coupons for weeks to get so many.

"Look! A torch!" Santie pulled it out of her stocking triumphantly and switched it on. "That's better, now we can see what we're doing."

Sated with toys, mouths full of sticky sweets, Santie wound up the little dog, holding its middle, idly watching its legs running in the air.

"I know! Let's put it on the table, see if it works." Jumping up, flashing her torch around the room before tucking it under one arm so she could wind the dog up again and set it going. As he clanked across the table, Santie cried "Look, Lou – look! Its head's moving as well!" On the steel surface the dog made such a racket we were scared it'd wake Mum and she'd come down and tell us off, it still being dark and all.

"Cor, doesn't it make a row? Better wait till we get up. Put it back in your stocking for later," and Santie giggled back into bed.

The next thing I heard was Mum saying, "Come on sleepyheads and Happy Birthday Santie dear. Ah, I see Father Christmas has been, got here then, in spite of the blackout. Get up now I've got a treat for you both – a real boiled egg! Mrs G over the back's chickens obliged and she let me have a couple special when I said you were coming up for the holidays. Wasn't that kind? After that we'll open our presents together."

More presents? I hadn't emptied the stocking yet although most of its contents were already strewn over the eiderdown. Then I remembered that for weeks we'd been making Christmas presents in Sewing at school, so that must be what Mummy meant.

I'd got bookmarks for Mum and Dad, made out of a strip of cotton canvas, one end folded into a point, laboriously blanket-stitched all round in coloured wool with B-O-O-K-M-A-R-K in wavering letters down the middle. Despite my tiresome twitch, I liked and was already quite proficient at doing simple embroidery.

"It's very good for her age," Mrs Moffatt – whose class I had moved up to, tearfully leaving adored Miss Digby's – reported to Aunty, just stopping herself from adding, "considering she's left-handed" like most silly old grown-ups did.

Uncle and Gramps got some more spills, strips of tightly twisted paper tied round the middle with an odd piece of ribbon from the ragbag, to light their pipes with from the fire and save matches. Aunty made a little needle case from tiny squares of felt, too fiddly a task for my fingers, for me to give to Santie. But a tassel hung from it, looped round in embroidery silks twisted together, which was All My Own Work. Sant's birthday coming the same day worried me for a while until Aunty suggested I 'bought' some pretty glass-headed pins from her workbox, putting a halfpenny in her Church Fund Box in payment.

"*That's* for Christmas," I squealed at Santie, as she unwrapped my gift, "and inside," nearly snatching it off her in my eagerness, "*they're* for your birthday. Do you like it? Aren't you pleased?"

Later that morning, after being made to sit quiet and look at a book for a while as all the excitement was making my twitch worse, wearing new winter frocks which Aunty had made secretly and packed in our cases in a sealed packet with a label on saying, 'GIVE TO MUMMY, DON'T OPEN YOURSELVES' we set off to walk to the Harrises in air so cold our breath streamed out into the brilliantly blue and sunny sky.

Santie and I carried little cloth bags with our slippers and pyjamas in; I'd been told we were staying the night. This meant that as well as taking presents, Mum and Dad had to carry our rations, enough for two days. Even if you only went to a friend's house for tea you always took your portion of butter or marge, sugar and tea with you plus anything else you could spare; fruit, a pot of home-made jam maybe or like today, one of Mum's cakes.

"All grist to the mill," Mum said, "although I was a bit short of ingredients for that cake; looks as if I stood the other end of the kitchen and threw the currants in one by one! Still, better than nothing, eh?"

The Harrises lived about two miles away, no distance at all really for Santie and me, used as we were to the long hilly walks to school every day. They had a huge rambling house exactly halfway along a winding uphill road; just as you thought I can't go another step, there you were.

Although older than Mum and Dad they had been close friends since before the War. Daddy, always a steady and careful cyclist, one day misjudged a right turn, caught his front wheel in the tramlines and came off in the middle of the traffic. Though unhurt, the shock of hitting hard ground brought on a very bad asthma attack and the crowd that gathered, frightened, called an ambulance.

Dad came to in an unknown London hospital and in the bed next to him, nursing a broken arm, was Mr Harris. Having the same interests, music and cycling, they hit it off from the start and when it was found they lived only a couple of miles from each other, well that put the tin hat on it, Dad said.

Never having much sense of direction, the first time Mum went to visit Daddy she got a bit lost and asked a woman who got off the bus with her if she knew where the hospital was.

"That's funny, I'm going there myself to see my husband," she said. "You come along with me. We can walk from here, it's not far."

They got chatting about their husbands, who turned out to be in the same ward. Yes, of course, the lady was Mrs Harris.

"From that moment," Daddy told us, "we were meant to be friends. God was watching and knew we'd all get on like a house on fire. I just wish He'd thought of a less painful way for us to meet than hitting that blimmin' tramline!" And friends we all remained over the next twenty years or so.

They understood about Dad's illness, knew he and Mum wouldn't go out much because he dreaded being taken bad in a strange house.

"Come round anyway, my dears," Mrs Harris would insist. "And if Jim doesn't feel too good when you get here he can rest quiet for as long as he likes. You're more than welcome, you know that, we love having you here."

In spite of the freezing weather the Harrises' front door stood wide open; inside and out a crowd of grown-ups, children and a little yappy dog which I didn't like, were milling about shouting, laughing, hugging one another. As we came up the path, several people detached themselves and calling out greetings, swept us in among them. Sucked as usual into a forest of legs, loving hands grabbed Santie and me, planting unwanted kisses on us, trying to pick me up. Overwhelmed and frightened, I clung to Santie, hiding my face in her cold woolly coat.

"She'll come round in a minute, won't you duck? When she gets used to you all – you know what she's like with strangers," Mum was saying, briskly unbuttoning my coat and leggings, shoving slippers on my reluctant feet. I wanted to go home, back to Aunty May and Uncle Fred and Ginger and Gramps, where it was safe.

The Harrises. Wonderful, warm, loving people, so glad to see everyone, filling their home with friends and neighbours.

"If we've got it, you can have it," was their motto, as they poured out drinks and handed round 'the horse's doovers' as Mr Harris called it and everyone roared.

After a while, when most of the crowd melted away and thankfully the yappy dog went too, I let go of Santie's hand and ventured a smile round at the beaming grown-ups that remained.

That Christmas Day turned out to be the happiest I have ever spent, before or since. People came and went throughout the day and night, and the party continued till the following evening. Every arrival got such a rapturous welcome that Pat, Santie and me, too excited to sleep, spent the night chasing up and down in our dressing gowns. The party started up again with each new peal on the doorbell and, so as not to miss any of the fun, we abandoned the cold attic bedroom and slept when we wanted to, anywhere.

"Harry's got home, wasn't expected to, that's why they're making such a fuss," Santie said, shortly after our arrival, as we climbed the stairs behind Pat, the youngest, a little older than me, to put our night things in one of the big attics that ran the width of the house. Now it seemed only Santie and I would stay the night. Mum and Dad said they had to go home, to feed Blackie and because Dad was on Standby for Fire Watching.

Alarmed, imagining we'd been tricked and I'd never see them or Aunty May again, I squeaked,

"They won't leave us here for ever, will they?"

Santie snapped,

"Course not, silly," then added, with her impish grin, "Anyway I know the way back so if they do forget *I'll* get us home toot sweet." (She was doing French at school).

"Who's Harry?" I asked Pat as we went down again, "are all these people your uncles and aunts?"

"No," she laughed, "he's my brother, they're all my brothers and sisters – well, most of 'em. Mum says I'm 'the afterthought'. Harry came home on forty-eight hours' leave last night and brought a couple of pals with him as well. Freddy might be home tonight, he sent a telegram and Mum's counting on it of course. Nell's on late turn, she's asleep at the moment. Her bloke's coming round later on, Bob, he's nice. Sh-h-h, this is her room, mustn't wake her." We tiptoed past one of the doors, then hurried on round another corner, down more stairs, another landing and all the while Pat chattered on.

"Vi's here, just for the day, got to be back tonight. Bert's home for good because of his foot. Mum's pleased he's out of it but Beatie doesn't know whether she's glad or sorry well, glad he'll be all right of course."

"Bert?" Grasping at a word in her endless flow of names, struggling to follow the breathless recital.

"Beat's husband. She's the eldest and I'm the youngest. All the rest are 'in-betweens'."

"Did he hurt his foot then?"

"Got blown off. Come on, your sister's down already, beaten us to it. Dinner's nearly ready, goody. I'm starving, aren't you?"

Chapter Nine

"Just look at it, coming down in stair-rods." Aunty May tutted out of the kitchen window, emptying the washing-up bowl into the sink with a flourish so the water joined the rain that had overflowed the gutter and it all swilled down the drain together. "On a Saturday too, what a shame. I had a picnic all planned for today, after it being so lovely yesterday. That's off for a start; even if it eases up it'll be too wet to sit anywhere. What d'you think, Fred? Will it clear?"

Uncle Fred was in the conservatory which adjoined and ran parallel with the back room and part of the kitchen. The kitchen door led directly into it instead of straight into the garden, so you had to go through the conservatory door as well to get out of the house the back way. Every morning after breakfast Uncle Fred could be found under the sloping glass roof, absorbed with his plants. Gently nursing one of his 'specials', tapping a pot, poking a finger into another's soil, all the while sucking his teeth as he worked slowly along the wooden shelves.

I loved the conservatory; its thick glass muffled all but the loudest sounds and when you spoke your voice was all funny and flat. A warm, buzzy comfortable place, full of the sharp green smells of leaves and moisture; even on a wet day like today, with the roof vents shut, you didn't feel cooped up at all.

Aunty didn't know that one of our favourite treats was having tea in the conservatory. This came about one afternoon when Aunty's friends were coming round and they wanted to talk about serious, grown-up things privately, with no little ears eagerly flapping. Aunty put it to Santie that instead of sitting with them, this time wouldn't we rather have a tea-party all by ourselves at our very own table in the conservatory?

82

Santie knew instinctively this arrangement was initially for Aunty May's benefit but her quick mind saw it could be turned to our advantage if she only had a chance to think about it. Aunty had sprung the idea on her so suddenly Santie had no time then to work out all the ultimate benefits. So she paused while Aunty gazed at her anxiously, before nodding slowly, saying,

"Well, all right then, I suppose so."

Knowing nothing of this conversation and dawdling into the hall one morning during school holidays I was surprised to see Aunty's ample bottom filling the doorway of the Glory Hole as she bent over, helping Sant to lug the card-table out from under the stairs. Santie winked at me, mouthing,

"Tell you later," putting her finger on her lips. Turning she said loudly into the cupboard,

"Oh good, Aunty, here's Louise come to help."

We dusted the table and set it up in the conservatory with our favourite cloth on but the plain everyday china as it wasn't such a disaster if accidentally broken. Not that we were careless mind, but if you dropped anything fancy on the stone floor it didn't stand a chance, unlike the thick carpet in the back room from which many a bouncing cup or plate had been rescued intact.

When tea was ready we went tidily in to shake hands politely with the visitors before melting away into the kitchen, choosing what we wanted to eat from the goodies Aunty laid out especially for us. She poured our tea from the old brown everyday teapot. When we wanted a refill Santie knocked on the window behind us, demanding imperiously,

"More tea, please," whereupon Aunty excused herself and bustled out to the kitchen.

Occasionally the visitor sitting nearest forestalled her by getting up smilingly to push the window open, saying,

"I'll do it, May, you stay there," taking our cups in. Not knowing about our private kitchen arrangement, she filled them from the second-best china pot that matched the teaset they were using. I found 'Visitors' Tea' rather weak for my taste and it smelt a bit flowery, too.

Although normally we did Aunty proud, were well-behaved and didn't show her up, every once in a while just for devilment we'd go too far, particularly if the guests included someone we didn't like much. Then Santie knocked two or three times for refills, though we were full up to bust, for the pleasure of seeing the grown-ups dance attendance on us at each summons, while we lolled back in the Lloyd Loom basket chairs.

In a rash moment Santie told Mum about our tea-parties and Mum got angry, indicating Aunty thought we weren't good enough to sit at the same table as "her stuck-up friends" and she'd give May a piece of her mind. Santie begged her not to as we loved having tea on our own better than anything. Mum must have held her tongue for once as we continued to rule the conservatory roost whenever Aunty's friends came to tea.

"Fred!" Aunty called again, "didn't you hear me? I said is this rain ever going to stop?"

Uncle Fred came reluctantly to the conservatory door where I was loitering, picking at a sliver of loose wood on the frame. Gently stroking my head as we stood side by side in the doorway he looked at the leaden sky and sodden fields then slowly shook his head,

"No, Mare, can't see any breaks. Mind, it could be lifting a bit over there," pointing at the top of Mrs A's paddock. "Might clear by dinner time but I wouldn't bank on it," and with a final soft pat on my hair he returned to his plants.

"H'm, doesn't sound too hopeful. I suppose we could go to the Pictures. Louise, you were in there last – can you remember what's on?" Aunty smiled hopefully at me but I shook my head. She looked doubtfully at the rivulets of red mud running down towards the back door then said,

"Where's Santie? SANTIE! Come here, I want you for a minute!"

"She's gone in to Mrs A with the things for Elizabeth," I said helpfully. Elizabeth was only about three, yet anything I grew out of that still had some wear in it went next door in the hope it would come in handy for her some day. What Mrs A did with this or whether she even wanted it was anybody's guess, for I never saw Elizabeth wearing any of my cast-offs when she got bigger.

"Of course, now I remember – I didn't want both of you paddling in and out in this weather. Well in that case Pieface you'll do instead. Got your wellingtons on? Good. Run and see what's on. Be quick and try not to splash up, there's a good girl."

Delighted, I dart out the door, jumping the puddles and into the outside lavatory. This whitewashed edifice separated the end of the kitchen from the big coalshed and all three adjoined one other. Although Aunty's house looked completely square from the front, round the back it was L-shaped. The short bit of the 'L' was the end wall of the dining room and hall while the long side contained the back room, kitchen and the two outbuildings.

You were only really supposed to use the upstairs lavatory at night, or if you weren't very well or if the weather was bad. Otherwise you went in here but I didn't mind as it was quite a nice place to sit and think undisturbed. The walls were completely covered in framed sepia photographs of 'known beauty spots' in Cornwall and Devon, some of them in villages not far away from us, like Cockington Forge. You saw pictures just like them in the railway carriage when you got on the train.

You could have a nice read if you liked because the lavatory's polished wooden seat had extended sides and old copies of *Woman* and *Woman's Weekly* were piled on them.

Strung on the wall facing the seat were posters from the cinemas in Newton and Torquay. I never discovered how Aunty got hold of them, because other people's lavs didn't have cinema posters like ours. Every week a new one arrived so

they were always up to date. When there were too many for
the string, Aunty took them down and cut then into small
squares which were hung next to the chain 'for the
Necessaries'.

Staring now at the top poster I yelled over my shoulder
"IT'S A U! MISSIS MINERVERRAR!"

"Where?"

"In here, on the wall!" I shouted back.

"Whatever's the matter with the child, must be all this rain,"
Aunty muttered, then called, "Yes, I *know* – is it Newton or
Torquay?"

"BOTH!" I screamed. "Shall I tell you who's in it?"

"Don't stand there shouting, you're getting soaked dodging
about in the door like that. Come in and bring the poster with
you."

But it was too high up for me to pull down without tearing
and as I scrabbled hopelessly at the wall Santie's running feet
came splashing round the back. She stopped, looked in and
said,

"What on earth are you doing? I could hear you shouting
right down by the front gate."

Aunty called out,

"Ah, you're back Santie dear; tell me what's on – I can't
make head nor tail of what Louise is saying."

"Let me see then," pushing me to one side. "Mrs Miniver-
Greer Garson-Walter Pidgeon-John Hodiak-doors open 12.40.
It's a U. Can we go? Isabel's seen it, says it's lovely."

Running and jumping through the back door, kicking off our
boots, we rushed wetly into the huge rough kitchen towel
Aunty was holding out for us. Rubbing our wet heads, she said
mysteriously to Santie,

"Is it suitable for You-Know-Who?" who nodded
importantly. "Pictures it is then so we better have something
quick for dinner. I was going to do sausage and chips but it'll
take too long – though how it can call itself a sausage I'll never
know, all bread and bits these days. There! You're dry, you

two, but run and change now so we don't hang about after dinner. And Louise!" Aunty shouted as we raced off down the hall, "put your apron on when you come down and try and stay CLEAN!"

"I'm glad it's not chips," Santie said when we were in the bathroom, "Aunty's are all soggy and she grumbles when she bends down in front of the fire and they never go brown no matter how long she shakes them about. Now *Mum's* chips are out of this world!" and she rolled her eyes, patting her stomach at the memory.

Aunty had an electric cooker in the kitchen and next to its plug the letters 'ON' and 'OFF' had been cut out from the *Daily Mirror* headlines and stuck on the wall by the switch. Because you had to save electricity like everything else, she only used the cooker for a short while each day. So Aunty mostly cooked over the fire in the back room, crouching down to stir the pan that was balanced on the little iron shelf hooked at the front of the fire basket. This worked well for vegetables or boiling a kettle if you weren't in a hurry, but it was no good trying to fry anything complicated as it took so long to heat up the food went all mushy.

The range had a big oven next to the fire in which Aunty baked meatless pies and stews, or did baked apples and in the winter Ginger and I sat on the red polished hearth tiles with our backs against its warm front, Ginger snoozing while I stumblingly read aloud to her.

A sizzling bacon smell came floating up the stairs and Santie and I nudged each other giggling, splashing water around in our hurry to finish first. She always won of course and after asking,

"What d'ya bet? Fried bread, tomatoes or powdered egg?" she darted off without waiting for an answer, shouting, "Hurry up! Put on your peach dress and don't forget your apron!" before flying down to see if she'd 'won'.

The *peach* dress? I thought that had gone in to Elizabeth. It was still too small under the arms even though Aunty May had widened the armholes and made new brown lace sleeves for it. It was tight across its smocked front as well but, putting it on, I remembered the last time I wore it 'for best' and the feel of its satiny shine that I fingered all the way to Church that Sunday evening.

Sitting quietly between Aunty May and Santie, letting the vicar's droning voice drift over my head into the raftered ceiling, I made flowers and baby-in-its-cot out of my hanky and pondered. The lady in the pew behind had leaned forward to put her hymn-book down and I got a whiff of Phul-Nana, just like Mummy used. What puzzled me was instead of Mum's face, a railway station came into my mind.

Oh, I remember – it was when Santie and I came back to Devon after that wonderful Christmas of parties and bombs and Morrison shelters. Just as I'd got used to Mum and Dad's way of doing things and being in London here we were at Paddington, saying goodbye again.

Mum bent down to kiss us. The musky scent of her face powder whiffed over me, lingering for a moment before being overpowered by the steamy sooty air of Platform One. She'd altered her old winter coat by adding wide fur cuffs and matching collar which tickled my cheek softly.

"Mum looked smart, didn't she?" Santie remarked, pulling hard on the window strap to shut out the billowing steam from the engine after we'd waved and waved until we couldn't see Mum and Dad any more and the platform was left far behind. This time we weren't in the guard's van like parcels but, as proper little ladies, were travelling in the third class Ladies Only carriage.

"I wonder where she got the fur from," Santie was taking off her hat and gloves, unbuttoning her coat, motioning me to do the same. "I'm sure Daddy couldn't run to a fur coat and if Mum did have one by any chance you wouldn't cut it up to sew pieces on another coat, would you?"

"I expect it was in Trimmings with the bits for hats and you don't need coupons for hats," I said with authority, feeling very

grown-up. Santie was talking to me as if I was Isabel and
aware of the honour and being sensible for once, I worked hard
to keep the conversation going.

"Yes, but fur's different, you'd need tons of coupons even
for little pieces of it," Santie said. "It'd take *years*, probably
for ever."

As well as food and coal and petrol being on ration, even if
you were well off you couldn't just buy things like shoes and
clothes either unless you handed over special coupons as well.
Each item would be marked with the amount of coupons
needed, next to the price. Everybody in Britain was issued
with clothing coupons, the same as we all had ration books.

Posters at stations and advertisements in Aunty's magazines
urged us to be like 'Mrs Sew-and-Sew' and keep making new
things out of old clothes. If you were really desperate for
something but hadn't enough coupons left to buy it then and
there, you just had to save up your ration from week to week or
'borrow' some from a friend, praying the shop wouldn't sell
what you had your eye on in the meantime.

I thought hard for a while, then said,

"Aunty May had a fur coat. I saw it in her wardrobe, ages
ago, but it's not there now. I mean it was snowing when we
left Newton, we were freezing, but she didn't wear it to the
station to see us off, did she? She had on her Dark Green
instead."

We stared at each other as the light slowly dawned.

"She's cut it up, I bet she's cut it up and shared it out with
Mum!" Santie crowed with delight. "Probably the last time
they came down. I bet when we get back Aunty's coats have
all got fur on!" And we fell back on the scratchy seats,
shrieking and throwing ourselves around in the as-yet empty
carriage.

Suddenly the hanky was whisked out of my hands and I was
being nudged from both sides. People were shuffling their feet,

coughing, preparing to stand up. The Reverend Dyer had finished and was saying,

"Hymn number 176 – 'How Sweet the Name of Jesus Sounds,'" and Uncle Fred had already left the pew and was standing with the other Sidesmen, holding a collecting plate.

Mr Wilson crashed out the first two bars on the organ, nodded ferociously into his mirror at the choirboys and off we went, thankful the service was nearly ended, duty done and we'd all be let out again, any minute now.

Uncle's friend (Old 'Uncle' Bill) appeared in the aisle and the plate passed from hand to hand. Whilst still singing, both Aunty May and Santie glanced down a twisty-mouth warning at me and I beamed back, nodding. They always did this. It meant "leave it where it is!"

The first time I ever went to Sunday School with Santie, to stop me dawdling on the way home she took my hand and inside my glove was a penny.

"Why've you still got your penny?" Santie asked sharply. "You know Aunty told you to do EXACTLY what I did. Why didn't you put it in the plate when it was passed along?"

"I did put it in," I protested, "but the plate came back again full up and stopped in front of me so I thought they didn't want mine and took it out again!"

Santie stood quite still and stared at me in disbelief.

"You took it *out*? Now what shall we do? I suppose we ought to go back to the Church and give it to somebody there but that'll make us late and Aunty'll be cross. Oh goodness me, what will Aunty May say?"

Suddenly she snorted, hand over mouth, then burst out laughing which set me off although I didn't know what was so funny. We giggled all the way home where Santie, taking and handing over my penny, told Aunty what I'd done. Aunty, mouth screwing up, told Uncle Fred and Gramps, who laughed so much that Santie and I started up again. I'm sure anyone passing in the lane must have heard us and wondered what was going on.

"Well, Pieface," Aunty recovered her breath and gave me a hug, "I can't say anything can I, not when it's all done in innocence. But in future you MUST leave the penny in the plate, even if they beg you to take it back which they won't, no fear of that, you say NO!"

Standing apart with Santie in the dazzling light of the setting sun, listening to the rolling Devon voices of Uncle Fred talking quietly with the Verger and 'Uncle' Bill, waiting for Aunty May to break away from Miss Crouch and Mrs Benson by the lych-gate so we can all go home, not for the first time I started wondering how God was going to get the pennies and sixpences Uncle and his pals collected. All the plates were put on a table by the altar and Mr Dyer held his arms over them, booming upwards a prayer about our offerings and His Good Works, with his eyes shut.

There were many, rather frightening, coloured pictures in my Holy Bible: old men in long dresses with flowing beards, something called 'a Prophet' turning walking sticks into hissing snakes; Jesus doing Miracles like curing mad people and raising the dead (terrifying pictures those, I'd turn the pages quickly trying not to look); or walking on the water in a blaze of light, while the fishermen's tiny boat tossed about in a terrible raging storm. But there was one I quite liked, of St Paul escaping from prison by being lowered in a large basket from his cell to the ground.

A basket! Of course, that's how it's done. God has a big basket and He lets it down on a piece of rope at the back of St Mary's. Mr Dyer tips each plateful into the basket, gives a tug on the rope and up it goes back into Heaven.

Feeling very pleased at having worked it all out and Aunty coming towards us holding out her hand while still half-turned to her friends so she sort of sidled up the path, I resolved we should all go and see this exciting event before the Verger shut up for the night.

"Can we go round the back and see the basket Aunty please?" Tugging at her hand, hopping on one foot, trying to turn her on to the side path.

"What basket? What's the child talking about, do you know?" looking at Santie, who shrugged.

"Search me!"

"Santie, I've told you before about talking in that silly way and here of all places. You're not in school now and I won't have it. Now Louise, I don't know about any baskets and it's time we went home, it's nearly your bedtime," and Aunty grasped my hand and marched me firmly through the gate.

"The basket with the money for God," I insisted. "Mr Dyer puts the money into God's basket and it goes up to Heaven."

Aunty actually stopped in the lane and stared down at me in complete bewilderment.

"I really don't know where you get these silly ideas from. Of course it doesn't go up to Heaven, you ninny; it goes into the bank in Newton and is used for the Church. I don't want to hear another word about baskets or money, do you hear?" And she fairly flew along the lane still holding my hand so I had to run beside her, frightened my arm would be pulled out of its socket.

Whatever Aunty May said, I clung stubbornly to my idea of God's basket, convinced I was right. I would go round the back by myself to see – one day soon, when I am a big girl like Santie and can go to Church on my own. Better to keep quiet for the moment though so until the new plan could be carried out it went into the slot inside my head marked SECRET. And there it remained.

Chapter Ten

Aside from Sunday School, we didn't always go to St Mary's. Aunty May spread herself religiously quite widely and several neighbouring village church-plates benefited from her largesse.

Buckfast Abbey was the Big Treat and we only went there on special occasions. The monks were actually building it and watching them go back and forth, carrying bricks, climbing ladders, calling cheerfully to each other above the noise and hammering was very exciting. I'd never seen anything being built before and fidgeted about during the seemingly endless services, longing to escape outside and resume my watchful interest in the busy, dark-robed figures.

There was a shop nearby where you could get candles and pictures of a laughing fat Baby Jesus and His Mother, statues and bibles and shiny crosses on beaded necklaces. Aunty bought me a hinged silver locket the size of a broad bean with a tiny red 'glass' window on the front; when you opened it there was a minute ivory figure of The Virgin Mary inside. The locket was meant to hang on a chain but I carried it in my purse, never tiring of opening the hinge to take out the statue, the envy of my schoolmates.

When I showed this treasure to Mum she frowned, saying she didn't hold with that sort of thing.

"May can do what she likes but I'm not having all this religious nonsense poured down the throats of *my* children," was her reaction. By this time I had learnt there could be disadvantages in telling my mother *everything* that went on at Aunty's so I said nothing about the books of Prayers for Little Folk, with their sickly pictures of smiling infants being Good, which appeared regularly on the top of my side of our chest of drawers.

Mum's fears were groundless anyway as I much preferred 'Pip, Squeak and Wilfred' in Aunty's weekly paper. In fact I read everything that came my way whatever its content, from the old copies of *Woman* and *Woman's Weekly* in the outside lav to the Church Magazine and instructions on packets of dried food in Liptons. Santie and I knew most of the advertisements on the bus off by heart and we'd chant them at each other, scoring points if you got it word-perfect. I won every time. It was the only thing I could beat Santie at.

My voracious reading appetite knew no bounds for one magical day at school Mrs Moffatt had a big sack on her desk and she tipped out lots of letters from children in America. We were told to choose a letter, read it and send our own letter to the writer, telling them about England. I picked one from a girl in Bangor, Maine called Mary Parsons and we corresponded for years. Mary came from farming stock, had nine older brothers and sisters and several large dogs. She regularly sent me her sisters' exciting American magazines for girls, much too old for me though I lapped them up eagerly. Thus began my lifelong love for America and the American people.

Santie longed for the clothes girls had on in the illustrations, 'jigger coats' that swirled round you, short flared skirts and trousers they called 'slacks'. Every girl had short socks on though, just like we did. These books were strict on how girls should behave, telling all 'Co-Eds' to Buy War Bonds, Do Their Daily Dozen, Take a Daily Shower to stay fit and healthy thereby helping Our Boys Win the War.

Some of these words took a lot of puzzling out. There was a man on the Pictures called Ward Bond and I suppose he wanted you to buy a ticket at the cinema. They'd just spelt his name wrong, that's all. And Co-Ed was the way you spelt CODE in American, to stop the Germans reading it. I gave up on a Shower and a Daily Dozen and asked Aunty May.

After much cogitating we settled on a brisk walk in the rain, wrapped up warm in your mac and wellingtons, and practising your Times Tables every day till you knew them by heart.

Aunty did that funny squeezing with her mouth when I mentioned the Code, said she wasn't sure about that and promised to write to Mrs Parsons and ask her exactly what it meant, likewise the mysterious 'Girl Scouts' that turned up some weeks later. Mary always finished up her letters 'God bless'; early on in our correspondence she mentioned her family said a special prayer for us and everybody in England every Sunday. So it was no surprise that Aunty May was all for Mary and her parents.

"She writes just as well as you do and her spelling is much better than yours," Aunty said approvingly. "You must keep up with them, who knows, you might get invited to America one day! They seem to be good people, even though they're farmers. Yes, Pieface, that's what 'small-holding' means, just like Mrs A next door. How strange it is: here we are, half-way across the world, and they're just the same as you and me."

Aunty made sure I put 'God bless' too every time I wrote to Mary although I didn't understand how God could be in America at the same time as keeping an eye on me in Devon.

St Peter's, in the hamlet on the other side of The Road, was another favourite church except it was really too long a walk for my short legs. From our bedroom window you could see doll-size houses at the top of the steep hill up which we gasped of a summer Sunday, frequently stopping and turning 'to admire the view'. Aunty's house got tinier and tinier the further we climbed, till it disappeared behind the hill. Snow White lived in the second cottage on the left at the top, though I never saw her, nor her Dwarfs, ever.

One side of the church was actually in a farmyard with staring cows around the muddy path through which you picked your way to get to the door and the all-pervading smell of pigs hung over the entire village.

The unusual thing about St Peter's – apart from the farmyard entrance – was because it was so small the bellringers had only a tiny recess at the back. They stood squashed together and you almost brushed the ropes hanging down on the left as you came in the door. If Aunty could be persuaded to sit in the back pew – difficult, as she thought this position rather beneath her – I could watch the ringers pulling on the fluffy coloured ropes, making the bells peal out bobs and changes. One by one the beautiful sounds faded until just the Calling Bell remained, rounding up the latecomers.

Then Aunty's gloved finger poked me sharply in the back and reluctantly I turned round to the same tiresome Evening Service as we had at St Mary's. That over, you faced the long walk home, skipping happily downhill until we crossed over The Road and started up the sharp incline to our house.

"Carry me, carry me," I'd whine, but everyone was tired by then and suddenly I was deemed "a big girl now, not a baby and anyway we're almost there."

At the end of the back garden, beyond Mr Miller's field and the railway line where the trains run to Totnes and Plymouth, hauling themselves up Dainty Bank (so steep it often needed an engine to push as well if more coaches or goods vans than usual were coupled on), lay another 'church' on our regular visiting list, the oddest of them all. This was a small chapel inside The Nunnery, an ugly grey building with a few bands of yellow and red bricks set high on its walls in an attempt to alleviate the overall gloominess of its facade.

Turning down a grassy track running parallel with the railway lines where I'd hang back by the fence hoping to see a double-header dashing through, the building loomed nearer and nearer until you reached its huge wooden door on which was fixed an iron bell-pull. When Aunty tugged at it a faint tinkling was heard and from directly above my head came a rattling, scraping sound. A small square hole appeared in the door with bars on it and through these a pale face looked out at us. It disappeared as quickly as it came, just like the Cheshire Cat in

Alice, then the big door opened and a silent nun beckoned us in.

Santie hated it, the nunnery, chapel, everything.

"They look as if they're locked up in prison, Aunty! How can they stand it? *I* couldn't. Don't let's go in, it's horrible," she'd plead. Aunty May would have none of it, urging Santie forward, telling her of course the nuns weren't locked up; they wanted to live in the nunnery, it was such a nice place to be and see how they smiled at us because they were so happy.

"You can tell how happy they are when you listen to their beautiful singing," Aunty whispered as we stumbled down the darkened corridor to the chapel. I liked the chapel very much and loved the singing, standing quietly, hardly twitching at all. Lit by hundreds of candles which gleamed softly on the many pictures and painted statues, it was like a larger version of Aunty's hated Shrine except here all was bright and colourful.

The goings-on were totally unlike St Mary's: little bells ringing and cupboards being opened and shut. Even though it all went straight over my head I was never bored – there was so much to look at. I loved the pungent smell of the stuff one of the two men in black gowns shook from a pot on a long chain. They did that in Buckfast Abbey too and chanted and sang in the same way though I didn't see any nuns there. But all this went on for so long I began to think Santie was right and the four of us would be shut up with the nuns for ever.

Gramps seldom came with us on these pious jaunts and only attended St Mary's now and then. Like my mother, he also thought Aunty May 'too churchy'.

"Are you coming with us today, Dad?" Aunty shouted every Sunday.

"Ay? What's that?" Gramps cupped his hand round his ear and pointed it in Aunty's direction.

"I think he's only deaf when he wants to be," she muttered. Then to Gramps, "I'm going to get you an ear trumpet next time I'm in town. Then there'll be no excuse."

She did too. It was a lovely thing, shaped like a small swan in black Bakelite. You put the neck bit in your deaf ear and the other person spoke into the body part. Gramps said he wasn't having no bloody ear trumpet like some old man, you could keep it. Aunty said he was nothing but an ungrateful old misery and the ear trumpet remained on the sideboard for ever more, dusted regularly every week along with the glass fruitbowl, Aunty's knitting bag, green candlesticks, ration books and wireless.

One evening Aunty lingered in the nunnery doorway, holding my hand, talking quietly among the rustling black gowns while my eyes watered from trying to yawn with my mouth closed. Santie etched patterns with her shoe in the gravelled forecourt, anxious to be off. They talked about me, I know, for Aunty tweaked my hand a couple of times and everybody smiled and nodded when I looked up. Then one of the men – Aunty called him 'Father', though he wasn't a bit like Daddy or even Gramps – bent down and put his hands gently either side of my face.

"Ah now, my little one," he sighed sadly. "Aren't you but one of the Lord's lame sparrows for us to take care of?"

At this, Santie darted back inside. Putting her arms round my middle she jerked me back out of his grasp, shouting loudly,

"My sister is NOT DAFT. She is VERY CLEVER and top of her class in school!"

"Ah sure, and she'll do well enough in this world with a champion like yourself to defend her!" laughed the Father as he straightened up. "No, no, not at all," he beamed at Aunty May, patting her arm. Poor Aunty was so stunned by Santie's unexpectedly rude interruption she was trying to tell her off and apologise to the priest at the same time. "She's a fine girl, protecting her sister, you must be proud of her."

Slightly mollified and smiling gracious goodbyes an embarrassed Aunty May hurried us out on to the gravel where Uncle Fred waited patiently.

"Father Gordon will be here in about three weeks, Mrs Sherwood, but the Sisters will let you know which Sunday for sure in good time, never fear," called the priest, as we all set off towards the lane. Santie looked like thunder though and when we were out of sight of the nunnery, she turned on Aunty May.

"What's Mum going to say?"

"That's between your mother and me and is not for you to question. Remember you're still a child and it's none of your business."

"You haven't asked her, have you? You know she'll say no. And it *is* my business, she's my sister. And what good will it do, anyway? But you needn't worry, I shan't tell Mum." Santie's mutinous face pinked up and she ran off ahead of us.

"Don't you be so cheeky, now," Aunty called after her, "speaking to me like that! I'll have a word with you, young lady, when we get home!" Aunty May looked unhappy and said quietly to Uncle,

"It won't do her any harm though and you never know, Fred, it might work. We can only hope and pray, poor old Tuppence."

And Uncle Fred smiled and nodded and patted the hand that she had tucked through his arm.

The next time we went into the chapel there were a lot more people there than usual. A nun stood at the arched entrance and after a whispered exchange with Aunty we were shown into the very first pew, right in front of the altar. This was a good start as the people who usually sat there got a wafer biscuit and a drink to wash it down, from a big glittery cup. I was very fond of wafer biscuits and looked forward eagerly to getting one at last. There was another priest as well, large and smiling, and at the end of the service he came and stood in front of me, completely blocking my view. Two nuns hovered either side of him.

One of the nuns softly touched my shoulder, murmured, 'Louise, St Vitus' Dance, Father,' and he bent forward, putting

"To Grace, from May"

Aunty's House

Aunty May and Uncle Fred

Sockless in Torquay

Off to Newton Market

"A bit of a blow"

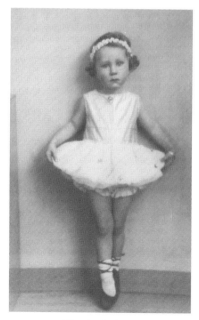

The little fairy

No cat calls today

"This one's for Mummy"

Uncle Fred's picnic Suit

The coveted ivory buckle

Aunty May by the village pond

" To May, from Grace"

his hands rather heavily on my head, holding it still. Aunty was fluttering advice by my side,

"Good girl, don't wriggle while Father Gordon blesses you."

But I hadn't sneezed. It was all very odd, although I was aware this special occasion was for me, to try and help my 'shakes'. I really believed I'd be cured, although Dr Black told Aunty there was no cure and I'd just grow out of it. When Uncle Fred wasn't well once, Dr Black said,

"I'd like a colleague of mine to take a look at you," and Uncle went to the hospital. Dr Black must have asked this new priest to take a look at me. I hoped I wouldn't have to go to the hospital too.

Father Gordon prayed loudly above my head and all around the chapel came a murmured chorus each time he paused. Then he said AMEN! and moved on to a lady further along the pew, who was fingering a necklace and muttering to herself.

Alas for Aunty's faith, my hopes and Dr Black's prognosis I never entirely grew out of it, twitching quietly on into my teens and beyond, slowly diminishing into today's imperceptibility. Come to think of it, I never got the wafer biscuit either.

In the Village, on the left side as you went up towards the bakers, were the Assembly Rooms where Santie was learning to be a King's Messenger. I wanted to be one too but of course was too young. I was always too young for everything that Santie was doing. However on a couple of occasions she unwillingly took me with her but I still didn't get to be a King's Messenger, for once inside the maroon-painted front door I was again abandoned with other infants while she went into the Big Class.

We all sat in a ring cross-legged on the floor, under instruction from Miss Webb. I did not like Miss Webb. She had a shrill voice and a toothy smile and I knew instinctively that Miss Webb did not like children. She tried very hard not to show it, bustling brightly round us, but her tightly-controlled patience gave her away.

Miss Webb told us more about Jesus and Miracles, pointing at the dim pictures around the room, telling us what He was doing in each one and what little sunbeams we'd be if we followed His example. It was a bit like being in Sunday School which was very jolly with nice Mrs Benson and sometimes Reverend Dyer was there; the pictures were prettier too. At Sunday School we sang about how the children 'made Sweet Hosannas ring', though who Hosanna was and why he wanted us to make him a ring I had no idea. You made rings from grass or straw, twisting and plaiting till it fitted your finger. Mrs Benson thumped heavily on the piano and taught us to 'Plough the fields and scatter,' which meant like playing 'Farmer's In His Den' – when Miss Digby called out,

"Scatter, children, find a space!" and you all ran off.

The second time I went to the Assembly Rooms with Santie, not so eagerly as before, Miss Webb asked if anybody knew what a parable was. Not expecting an answer she started to tell us. Well, I wasn't going to let her get away with that so I put my hand up.

"Louise? Yes dear, what is it?"

"I know what a parable is, Miss."

"No, of course you don't dear. How can you? After all, you're..." and she broke off with a little laugh and shook her head at me, as if I wasn't all there.

"But I do, Miss. I read it in a book Aunty gave me. It's 'an Earthly Story with a Heavenly Meaning.'"

Miss Webb stood stock still, staring down at me with her mouth open and her neck went a bit red. Then she smiled her tight bright smile and said,

"How clever of you and such a *little* girl too! Well, well, who would have thought it?"

Reading those Baby Jesus books had paid off, wouldn't Aunty be proud? What hugs I'd get when I told her!

Miss Webb was angry, I'd spoiled her story, made her look foolish. At that moment she disliked me more than all the others put together, I could feel it. I hated and feared her. She was the first grown-up I had met who wasn't friendly towards me and if this was learning to be a King's Messenger then Santie could keep it.

On the way home I told Santie how Miss Webb got cross because I knew what a parable was when she asked. Santie frowned, nodded and said "good girl" a couple of times but her mind was obviously elsewhere. When we got home she went into the kitchen to help Aunty do the cocoa and Aunty shut the door.

I couldn't hear more than murmuring but eventually Aunty said loudly,

"Yes, Santie, you did quite right to tell me – fancy, treating her like that! She shan't go again," and came through with the loaded tray.

"Don't you want to be a King's Messenger after all? Never mind, you're still my clever girl. I think this calls for a *real* biscuit – Santie, get the 'Blue Bird' tin down for me, there's a love. We'll have a treat instead of these lumps of concrete they're passing off as biscuits nowadays."

I was sorry that I wouldn't meet the King after all though. Why the King, the most important person in the world after God, had chosen my Santie to run messages for him was a constant wonder to me. I asked her about his messages – did she carry them in her satchel?

"Of course! He puts them in an envelope and gives them to the guard at Paddington every Friday and I collect them when I go to school on Monday morning." And she danced round me laughing while I stared at her, round-eyed with wonder, till Aunty told her to behave herself and stop teasing AT ONCE.

"You know she believes everything *you* tell her as though it's the gospel," Aunty said. In a way I suppose I still do.

Chapter Eleven

"Now children, quiet for a moment." Mrs Moffatt raised her voice above our clatter, noisily getting ready to go home. It was Friday afternoon and the bell had just rung and, much as I loved school, the bell's joyful clanging meant freedom to scramble on the sweetly-smelling hedgerows. The dog roses were out and I wanted to pick some for Aunty May. Usually their pink papery petals fell off as you dragged them from the hedge, flinching at each scratch from the sharp little thorns that covered their stems.

If a thorn actually got stuck in your hand then, when you got home with your bunch of almost petal-free roses, out would come The Needle, dipped in Dettol and, hand gripped tightly to stop you edging away, Aunty prodded painfully round your fingers. Honestly, that was worse than having something in your eye, when Aunty twirled the corner of her hanky into a turnip root and probed about to shift the bit of grit. These rather crude methods always worked though and you got a nice sweet from The Tin as a reward afterwards.

"Listen to me, children, before you go: whose mummies or daddies have got birthdays next week? Anybody? Brothers or sisters? Think now, quickly. Remember that person will make a birthday card in Drawing. Yes, Louise?" – for my hand was up and waving in the air urgently.

"It's Aunty May's next Wednesday, Mrs Moffatt."

"Aunty May's, eh? Well, you shall start the card in Monday afternoon's lesson then you can finish it on Tuesday if need be. And how old will Mrs Sherwood be on Wednesday, do you know?"

"Twenty-one!" I shouted, beaming happily at her but she just looked surprised.

"Oh I see, yes of course dear. Well, line up nicely at the door, Class, and I'll see you all bright and early on Monday morning. Goodbye and *quietly* out of school, please."

Useless injunction; let out at last we whooped and ran across the playground, rushing down the steps, all trying to squash through the gate at once.

"I'm going to make you a birthday card in Drawing next week, Aunty. It's a surprise. Mrs Moffatt said I was to. She asked how old you'll be on Wednesday and I told her."

Aunty May was in the kitchen cutting bread and scrape as I burst through the door with this exciting news. Her usual welcoming smile turned into a slight frown and she said, a little sharply,

"Oh *did* she – and what did you say?"

Now here was a puzzle and only proved yet again how odd grown-ups could be at times. When a new child started school or Aunty made you stand on the path with them after Church while she had a word with their mummies, the first thing you asked was "How old are you?" Even before, "What's your name then?" I knew everybody's age in my class, and Santie's and Isabel's.

"Twenty-one of course. That's what you told me when I asked the other day." Twenty-one was so very old that I couldn't imagine anyone ever being it.

Aunty May's mouth squeezed up again in that funny way she had sometimes.

"Well that's all right, Pieface, good girl. Yes, I did say that, didn't I? But you asked me a long time ago love, I'm surprised you've remembered all this time. Fancy Mrs Moffatt asking you, what a cheek she's got. Here, take this plate into the other room – wash your hands first, mind. We need some more jam so you can go and choose what you'd like for tea from the larder but hurry up, before Santie gets in."

Standing on a stool, washing my hands at the sink I glanced sideways at the doors to the two walk-in cupboards that made up the end wall of the kitchen, glad it was the larder and not the dark gloomy 'Hole' I was going in.

The Hole was full of brooms and buckets, mops and dusters hanging in a bag on the wall, rubber boots caked in red mud and old gardening shoes. A couple of ancient baize aprons with bits of twine and grass poking out of the front pockets dangled off a hook nearest the door. The leather shopping bag hung on the inside of the door and every time you reached in for it a smelly old mac wrapped itself round your head. Ugh, I hated that cupboard and if anything was wanted out of it I made sure I was nowhere to be seen.

The larder adjoining it was a cleaner, brighter place altogether. For a start it had a tiny 'window' with a piece of wire mesh fixed over it instead of glass, which overlooked the gravelled drive down which Santie and I had once rushed headlong in the old doll's pram. Its stone walls were painted white and there was a huge meat-safe fixed to the end wall facing the door. Even on the hottest day the whole pantry was icy cold.

Stone shelves ran along both sides, one with butter and cheese under mesh covers and fresh eggs from our hens in bowls. Santie and I didn't much like real eggs, preferring the National Dried Egg Powder you got as part of your ration from Liptons, when eggs were scarce. Even Aunty's rubbery omelettes tasted wonderful made with dried egg.

On the shelf under the little window Aunty kept the bottled fruit, jams and jellies she made from the soft fruit grown in the garden, when she could get enough preserving sugar (rationed, like everything else). Santie, Uncle Fred and I went blackberrying every autumn and these, added to our own apples, were turned into my absolutely favourite jam.

Uncle Fred and Gramps also pickled onions and made Very Hot mustard pickles from left-over vegetables. Great glass jars stood on the cold floor under the jam shelf, too heavy for me to lift though I frequently stubbed my toes on them rushing into the larder to fetch something Aunty had forgotten to get out.

Standing in the cold and airy pantry, I took so long reading the labels on the jars and making up my mind that Aunty, tired of waiting, called from the back room,

"Just bring the first one you come to for goodness sake, before you freeze to death in there!"

After supper that evening, I squatted under the raspberry canes to see if any were ripe yet because if they were I meant to eat my share now, while I had the chance. Last year Santie and I had two enormous strawberries picked to ripen for us. They sat on the slatted shelf in the conservatory growing redder and redder for a day or so till I could wait no longer and ate one. Delicious. Santie's strawberry grew fatter and riper when, ready at last, gloatingly she bit it. Alas, kept till it nearly reached bursting point, the fruit had gone rotten inside.

Crouched low, munching a juicy berry, Aunty's voice floated through the kitchen window opposite my hiding place, where she and Santie were washing up,

"And do you know what she replied? 'Twenty-one'! I didn't know where to put myself for a minute. Nosy woman! Just wanted to find out so she could gossip round the Village. Good old Lou; talk about out of the mouths of babes!"

Santie came laughing out the conservatory door to find me, calling "Bedtime!" – as if that would make me go in on such a warm, still evening. If she tried shouting, "Treacle Toffee!" I would have come running, like when you banged Ginger's dish with a spoon to get her in at night. So I stayed put, hoping my stealthy rustlings hadn't given me away. They had.

"You're pinching the raspberries Lou, how could you! Come out at once before anyone sees you. Gramps is coming down the garden and you know he'll tell Aunty, after what happened before. Quick now, quick!"

We certainly weren't in Grandad's good books – not that we ever were really. We'd done it this time though and Gramps wasn't going to let us forget it. Two or three weeks before, me and Santie were in quarantine. Chicken pox was rife at my school and although I hadn't caught it, Rose had. I had to stay home because of our close friendship and Santie's contact with me kept her at home too. Confined to the house and garden, unable to see our friends, we got on each other's nerves.

On the last Sunday of our enforced restriction, Auntie May and Uncle Fred took themselves off for a little evening stroll.

"We'll be back in half-an-hour at the latest," Aunty said as we went down to the gate to see them off. "Remember it's Sunday, so behave yourselves, no rushing about. Santie, you're in charge, find something quiet to do, the pair of you, and don't bother your grandad."

Knowing we'd be back in school tomorrow and out from under each other's feet at last, we were happy as sandboys. Hanging over the gate waving Aunty and Uncle off down the lane, left to our own devices for a short while we were ripe for mischief.

Strolling back up the drive we could hear Gramps stumping about in the coal shed. This large building, attached to the Outside, had two doors but only one was used, that next to the lavatory. The door giving on to the drive was locked and barred, otherwise you could have taken a short cut through the shed and avoided the uphill drag round the house to the back door. Which is why, apart from the fun of it, Santie used sometimes to get into the back room by climbing in the side window. Not me though, I was too little to scramble up and get a toe-hold so had to trudge round unless Uncle Fred lifted me through, to be clutched in by Aunty May.

Glancing in the coal shed as we passed, Santie asked cheerfully,

"Have you lost something, Gramps? Can we come and help?"

"You get away from here, you kids! I don't need your help. When I want it I'll ask for it!" Grandad glared at us from the doorway. He was rooting amongst the old furniture, boxes and garden tools that filled the front half of the shed, the coal being kept in an immense tidy heap at the back.

Santie bit her lip, her face flushed and I squeezed her hand sympathetically. Turning away we went to sit in the basket chairs in the conservatory.

"I wasn't being funny, Lou, honestly. I really thought he'd like us to help him. More fool me!" Santie flung down the latest American magazine Mary had sent me and jumping up, said,

"Come on! I'm going to pay him back, see if he wants our help then," and she ran outside and slammed the shed door tight shut, pushing the bolt across. Gramps was securely locked inside. Santie made a crowing noise, grabbed my hand and we ran to the top of the garden.

The sudden darkness engendered by the door closing alerted Gramps who, thinking a gust of wind had blown it shut, rattled the 'dupper' up and down. Nothing. Thump, thump. Silence. Wallop, wallop, wallop, followed by,

"Hoy! What the hell's going on? Let me out of here! I'll pay you, you little buggers, you wait till I get out!"

I was frightened by Grandad's shouting, realising that this time Santie had gone too far. Coming slowly down the path while Grandad continued shouting and hammering, she said,

"I suppose we should let him out but I'm worried he might hit us. He's so angry. I didn't think he'd be so angry. I thought we'd just bolt the door for fun 'cos he wouldn't hear us anyway and then we'd undo it again and he'd never know. It was going to be our secret. But it's all gone wrong and I don't know what to do. Gramps doesn't like me much at the best of times but he quite likes you."

By now we were standing outside the shed and Santie was looking uncertainly from it to me, real fear on her face. I knew at once she wanted me to open the door but I was too little to undo the bolt. So I said,

"You'll have to slide the bolt back Sant, it's too high up for me. Don't worry, Gramps can't hear you. I can reach the dupper though, so I'll open the door. It'll take him a minute to see he's free and we'll run down into the lane, wait for Aunty and Uncle. He won't chase us outside the gate and if he does we'll go in Mrs A's field, he won't find us in there."

Santie clutched me gratefully.

"You are a kind girl, Lou and I'm sorry I've ever been cross with you." It wasn't so much kindness, more that I knew how to 'disappear' when trouble threatened, knew where the safest hidey holes were, could work out our escape quickly and with ease while poor Santie dithered and fretted.

She stepped forward, hesitated then pulled back the bolt. All was quiet.

"Now, push the door open, Lou," she whispered, "I won't leave you on your own, I promise."

Safely out in the lane at last, pursued only by Gramps' voice bellowing all kinds of threats, we decided to sit on Mrs A's paddock gate anyway, just to be sure. Settling ourselves, Santie asked anxiously,

"Do you think he'll say anything to Aunty May? After all, it's his own fault really. If he hadn't been so nasty to me I wouldn't have shut him in."

"No, I expect he'll forget all about it," I lied, knowing full well we'd never hear the end of it.

And we didn't. He ranted on for days till Aunty said she was tired of hearing about it, whereupon he accused her of siding with us, taking our part – well, she always did when Gramps started on us – though she was extremely cross with Santie for leading me on, as she put it. Aunty meted out appropriate punishments which lasted a whole week: no playing out after tea for me and Santie had to wash up the supper things by herself. Her pocket money was stopped as well.

I never admitted it to Santie but really I was on Gramps' side, it was wrong what we did to him. Although only shut in for a few minutes, it must have felt like hours once the door slammed and trapped him in darkness – and silence, for he couldn't hear us coming to let him out. I kept saying I was sorry, trying to be friends, but he pushed me away.

I decided to make it up to him and it took a very long time to wheedle Gramps round. By following him about in the garden doing little tasks, asking questions about the vegetables, sitting on a stool by his side in the evenings and generally getting in his way, he gradually softened and began talking to me properly again.

One evening as I sat peering under his arm at the paper he was trying to read over the top of my head he said,

"You're trying to get round me, aren't you, you artful monkey?" and I said,

"Yes, Grandad, I am!"

Gramps barked his short laugh, rustled the paper at me as though shooing a fly away and said,

"Go on with you, but no more tricks mind, you and that sister of yours. I'm keeping my eye on you both from now on!"

Chapter Twelve

At the top of the garden, in the corner next to the chicken run where the boundary wall Mrs A's side joined our hedge with Mr Miller's field, was another shed. Wooden, small, whitewashed outside and in, it housed boxes of 'windfalls' – apples and pears too ripe or specky to be stored in the loft for the winter – and gave the shed a rich fruity smell. Unless the weather was really cold, Santie and I used it to play in and on hot summer days we had lemonade parties. Upon the apple-green door Uncle Fred had painted, in runny white letters, THE WHITE HOUSE.

Aunty let us have the remainder of an old willow-patterned coffee set, the tiny cups just the right size for our small fingers, and these were arranged tidily on the shelf along the right-hand wall. There were a couple of plates and some tiny spoons too but no saucers. The shelves on the left by the window were Uncle Fred's territory and held old jars and tins full of nails, screws, rusty bolts and hinges, keys to long-forgotten suitcases – in fact all the paraphernalia that was sure to come in handy the moment you threw it away.

We had two elderly kitchen chairs, their legs cut down to child height long before we ever came to Devon, just right for Santie and me. They stood either side of a small and rickety cane table, originally in the conservatory but deemed too disreputable to be on show, as it were. We kept some magazines and books and a few toys in a wooden box which also doubled as a spare table and spent many amicable hours together in the White House, Santie often doing her homework at the table after tea, quite undisturbed.

In sight of the kitchen door so we could be signalled at if wanted the shed became our private domain. Apart from Uncle coming in to collect windfalls for stewing and pies, nobody else, not even Rose or Isabel, visited the White House. Rain or shine, we played Snap and Happy Families or sat reading, embowered by the small orchard right outside the always-open door. Even on my own I was perfectly happy, playing at Grown-ups Taking Tea (little finger stuck out at the side of the cup) or showing Teddy the apples quietly rotting in their boxes, snuffing up their cidery smell and having a good nibble round at what was on offer.

Although not supposed to actually pick fruit off the trees ourselves, we could eat any that had fallen. If they were all maggoty, or the birds had got there first, Santie would take a quick reccy of the house and garden and, if no one was about, we shook a selected tree vigorously. One balmy October day, busily picking up several juicy Conference pears helped to the ground by this method, we heard an angry shout of,

"Oy! Wot you up to? Get away from that tree you little devils," and there was Grandad, fairly dancing by the back door, waving his arms at us. Dropping the pears in fright, we fled.

Against the wall, over which I would hang, standing on a large upturned flowerpot to get my arms on the top which was curved and smooth like a pigsty wall, was a very unusual peach tree. Some years before one of its drooping branches became entangled in a small neighbouring apple tree. The resulting fruit from this misalliance was fuzzy-skinned and peach-like, had the crisp bite and taste of an apple and a big peach stone in the middle. The apple tree, by the way, bore its normal load of sharp green apples with no trace of a peach anywhere on its branches. Uncle Fred's peach-apple tree was quite well-known round about and it was a good job I wasn't keen on peaches or there wouldn't have been anything left to show interested growers who occasionally came round.

Another peach tree, tied on to the back wall of the house, never did very much, occasionally bearing a few small sour peaches that never ripened. Uncle said it was too old so had it cut down, dug out and later filled the space with another long row of runner beans. One September weekend when Mum and Dad were down for my birthday and Santie and I brought in the beans we'd just picked for dinner, Mum said,

"You've had better luck with your beans this year than we have, May. Ours made a very poor showing. Oh that reminds me, I must tell you what Jim said, it's so funny, you'll roar."

Handing the basket of beans to Aunty, Santie and she settled down to string them and I perched on Mum's lap, eager to start roaring.

"Well, like I said, the beans didn't do too well. Last weekend when he was in the garden, I asked Jim to bring me in some. So he came in and said, 'I've picked all there were, Grace. Would you like them all today or shall we eat half now and the other one tomorrow?'"

Aunty, Santie and Mum screamed with laughter, Aunty flinging herself forward on to the kitchen table. Uncle Fred, sitting in the conservatory with Daddy, reading the paper, chuckled warmly and said,

"That's a good one, Jim," and Dad grinned back nodding.

I wasn't roaring, though. I laughed at everyone else doubled up but what was so funny eluded me. Had Daddy made one of his famous puns? No, people usually groaned when he did and here they were, busting their sides instead. It was too complicated for me, so I slid off Mum's lap and went off to the White House to try and work it out.

There were several things I didn't like and kept away from in the garden, like the pampas grass into which, running screaming down the steep front lawn during an exciting game, I once tripped and fell headlong. The sharp leaves left many little painful cuts on my arms and legs and I cried buckets. Uncle put a temporary string-and-stick barrier across but he needn't have bothered because I never went near the pampas again.

About midway between Mr Miller's field and our 'orchard' was the object I feared the most: a very deep well from which fresh spring water could be pumped up to come gushing out of the old iron pump standing by the path. Springs and wells abounded in our corner of South Devon and most of the villages round about bore some watery reference in their names.

The well was always covered with a thick wooden board, round and extremely heavy, on top of which was a big boulder. Very occasionally the cover would have to be removed but Aunty May gave Santie and me plenty of warning to keep out of the way, especially as she knew I was terrified and wouldn't go near it with the cover *on* even.

One day when Grandad had the cover off I deliberately went, though scared stiff, to watch him at work. Gramps saw me coming and instead of waving me away warningly, he held out his hand,

"I'm here, Tuppence," he said kindly, "there's nothing to be afraid of so long as you're with me or Uncle. You just hold tight to your old Grandad, he won't let you fall."

Shaking fearfully and clutching Gramps' jacket while he held me firmly in both arms, I stood close to the well and peered down at the dark green, fern-encrusted top from which a smell like an old wet flannel arose.

"There's a brave girl," said Gramps, drawing me away after a minute, back to the safety of the path. "You won't be scared of it anymore will you?" Oh yes I will, Gramps, I thought, though I smiled and shook my head. "All the same, you still mustn't come here on your own. Want to know how deep it is?" I didn't, I wanted to run off right then and there and never come back. "Here's a pebble, I'll chuck it in and you tell Grandad when you hear the splash."

Later, well safely covered up again, I watched Gramps pushing the squeaking pump handle up and down and waited for the water to shoot into the old tin bath, from which in turn he filled his watering cans.

"Where's that water got to?" Gramps said, "it's taking its time. Have a look up the pump, see if it's coming yet." He was grinning and chuckling and, although I could now hear the water rising, one more push would do it, I played his game, crouching down to stare up the spout.

Whoosh, splosh, all over my face. Very satisfying for Grandad, crying, "Whoops!" in pretended astonishment, chortling at my shrill squeaks, jumping smartly back, although I loved playing about with water. And to make grown-ups laugh at any of my antics was music to my ears.

Running into the kitchen, I shouted at a surprised Aunty May how I'd seen down the well, which was "*horrible* Aunty, ugh, all green and slithery." From my wet appearance for a terrible moment Aunty thought I said '*been* down the well' and clutching me to her yelled over my wet stringy hair what was he thinking of, had he gone completely off his head, at Gramps, still chuckling as he followed me in – until met by this onslaught.

Between us we got it all sorted out in the end, Gramps and me. Santie was round Isabel's when all this was going on so there was plenty to tell her when she got back.

"You never!" she gasped, though one look at my irritatingly smug face told all. She liked it best when the water came out over me until I admitted standing under the pump because I realised Gramps wanted me to get splashed. Santie's smiles faded and she looked at me thoughtfully.

"You're growing up Louise, beginning to latch on. Still, no matter how old you get you won't catch me up. You'll always be my little sister!"

Imitating Uncle and Grandad as they fought their weed-wars among the vegetables, I stood alongside helpfully, spade at the ready. When they loosened a tough weed to make it easier for me to lift, I crouched down, digging with alacrity, encouraged to use my seaside spade before it went rusty with non-use – at least, that's what Gramps said would happen.

Although many beautiful beaches were only a short bus-ride away in any direction except the one leading straight up on to Dartmoor, you couldn't play on them or paddle along the edge of the waves where seagulls dipped and screamed overhead because of the War, particularly the Enemy who from what I could gather preferred the seaside to anywhere else.

Sometimes a man in uniform stopped you even going near the steps that led down on to the sand. One day when he wasn't there, hurrying eagerly towards the steps we found boards blocking the way, tied to the rails at the top. So my bouncy seaside ball and little spade stayed at home, like Mummy and Daddy, 'for the duration'.

When Aunty May's special friend, Miss Crouch, came round for "a little chat, just the two of us, May" over a pot of tea, for which Aunty got out her best china set with the roses on and actually used the drawing room (Miss Crouch was very posh) I knew it would be worth hearing, to tell Santie later. Perhaps they'd talk about the War. Smartly though plainly dressed, well off, Miss Crouch was 'a real lady' and lived in a huge house, bigger even than ours, the other side of the Village. She was the nicest of Aunty's friends, always stopping to speak to me or Santie even when we were on our own.

Running in from school, sent to shake Miss Crouch's hand, who greeted me with pleasure, it was no difficulty to be winsome for a few minutes before Aunty, beaming with pride, steered me back to my tea, laid ready in the back room.

"Play quietly when you've had your tea, Louise and I'll call you when Miss Crouch goes to come and say goodbye nicely. Be a good girl now, don't let me down." Aunty bustled away and the drawing room door clicked shut.

Of course I wouldn't let her down! I'd be quiet as a mouse, Aunty mustn't know I'm even there. Golloping my tea down I crept to our 'listening post', the fourth stair up from the bottom where you could sit and hear people talking in the drawing room best, even with the door closed. As soon as their voices dropped to a murmur that was when to listen hardest and my ears, already sharp as any bat's, strained the most.

I heard about Mines and Landing Craft, how Mrs W managed they'd never know, especially with Another on the way and him away Poor Soul and what with the Gee Eyes and all – oh yes, plenty of them my dear, still about. A lot of this conversation seemed connected in some way with Torquay and Dawlish; Teignmouth also got a mention and once Newton did too.

I knew about mines, that was where the coal came from before it got into our coal shed or piled high at Newton Station to stoke the boilers, Uncle Fred said, so the engines could get up a good head before Dainty Bank. Landing craft was easy as we did Crafts at school, which was knitting and sewing. Aunty had Santie and me cut clean material into strips some winter evenings and showed us how you made a rag rug, too tough for us to do. So the landing craft must be a new rug for the landing upstairs.

Gee Eyes was a puzzle. I'd have to ask Santie when she came in. At the back of my mind was a vague memory of Miss Digby's cousins, the ones she stuck the flags on the map for, her Al-Eyes. Perhaps the Gee Eyes were Miss Crouch's cousins.

Movements within the room, cups rattling on to the tray, Miss Crouch saying what a *lovely* time she'd had and how sorry she was to miss Santie but she really must be going or Edgar would wonder where she was. Coming to with a start and not wanting to be caught eavesdropping ('ear-'oling' Lily called it) I shot up the stairs and out of sight just as Aunty called out,

"Louise! Ah, here she is – come and say goodbye to Miss Crouch, dear. You've been so quiet up there we wouldn't have known you were in the house! Have you been playing with your dolls' house?"

"Santie?"

She was in the conservatory, frowning at her knitting.

"Can I ask you something?"

"What is it *now*? Can't you see I'm trying to turn a heel? Do you have to keep bothering me all the time? I showed you how to cast off, you can't have forgotten already."

I could knit, just about. Miss Digby had shown us how in Class One and, using very big wooden needles, we struggled to plain and purl while the big woolly balls rolled across our desks, bomp-bomp-bomp on to the floor, winding round chair-legs, gathering fluffy dust on the way. Eventually the wool pulled so tight, sometimes broke, and Miss Digby made us get down to unravel it. Most knitting lessons ended with a group giggling about the floor, tangling the wool even more in our efforts at undoing and having a thoroughly silly and enjoyable game.

Unlike embroidery, knitting held little interest for me. When we moved up into Mrs Moffatt's, for one of the craft lessons each week (there was one nearly every afternoon of some sort or another) you could bring your own work. Having lied that Aunty May was continuing Miss Digby's woolly teachings at home, I contentedly chain-stitched and daisy-looped Aunty's Anchor stranded cottons on to ironed-on transfers on linen hankies.

I got caught out later though. Getting no further than endless straight rows, when Teddy's new green scarf was long enough to go twice round his neck and tie at the front, I just pulled it off the needles and broke off the wool. But it didn't look like proper knitting at all for the little loops started unwinding, faster and faster till Teddy's scarf was half the length.

Carrying this disaster to Santie, long wrinkled end of wool trailing, face quivering, starting to sniffle,

"It's gone wrong, Teddy's scarf!"

She took pity on me.

"Not like that, you ninny. Honestly, Lou, you're hopeless! You have to fasten it off, stop it undoing. Now you've got to knit it all up again, only this time leave it on the needles and I'll show you how to cast off."

Which she did, many tedious rows later, patiently repeating the procedure until I could cast off with the best of them.

Now, glancing up and seeing I'm empty-handed, she snaps,

"Well?"

"I wanted to ask you – I just wondered what Gee-Eyes meant, that's all."

"GI's? They're Americans. You know – 'corse you do," for I am shaking my head. "The soldiers, you've seen them in the Village. They were camped over on the Downs, you know, near where Miss Crouch lives. Oh, I get it – you've been listening at the door again, you'll get caught one day. What did she say then, about the GI's? No, stop a minute," as I start to speak, "not in here; the White House – come on."

Jumping up grinning, face alight with interest, Santie tosses her knitting on the basket chair and runs out the door after me.

One sultry morning some months before, I woke up early feeling as if the ceiling was sitting on my head. Rolled into a tight ball,

"It hurts, it hurts," I cried to Santie, who got up at once and fetched Aunty May.

"Does your head ache a lot, Pieface? You look very peaky, I must say. It's this blessed weather, too hot for me. Lie quiet then and I'll bring you some milk and half an aspirin. If you're no better by this afternoon I'll get Dr Black to have a look at you."

It certainly was hot, the overcast sky heavy with thick yellowy clouds, not a breath of air stirring the lacy curtains, although the bedroom window was wide open. I'd had headaches before and knew it would go if I kept still. Santie quietly got ready for school, tucked Teddy closer to my side and smilingly waggled her fingers at me round the door.

"I reckon we'll have a storm later on, shouldn't be a bit surprised." Aunty May fanned herself with the *Daily Mirror*, taking sips of tea. Roused from sleep by the telephone ringing down in the hall, headache all but gone, I got up at dinner time and now mooned around Aunty, rubbing my head against her silky knees until she said,

"Don't do that love, you're making me hotter than ever. I expect you're fed up with lying down, aren't you? Why don't you go into the garden? Don't run about though, you'll make yourself worse. You could go and sit on the gate. It's too early for Santie but you might see young Tom on the cart. Go and wave to Tom, why don't you? But promise me, don't go out in the lane though. Promise?"

Aunty had something on her mind. Ever since whoever had rung that morning she'd been preoccupied, smiling vaguely at nothing in particular. The telephone rang again as I wandered out and Aunty hurried to answer cheerfully,

"Yes, I heard, about time too if you ask me. No I can't come now, I've got poor Louise home, not well – no, nothing serious. We'll all get together later on, arrange some nice little social events for them."

Hanging over the gate, staring down the lane I wondered again why Tom didn't have white hair or stoop over like Gramps because he was deaf too. He only waved if he saw you but I was used to this. One day I heard clip-clopping hooves behind me as I came up the lane and scrambled into the bank while the cart lumbered slowly past, loaded with swedes. As the cart jolted over a bump a large swede rolled off the top of the pile and fell in front of me.

I ran to tell Tom, calling out and pointing as I drew alongside, but he just waved his hand in acknowledgement, smiling down at me from his great height, sat up behind the horse's huge wide bottom. Unable to explain I watched them rumble away and without turning round Tom again waved, above the back of his head. Returning to pick up the fallen swede I thought oh well, I tried didn't I, now it's mine. Licking my hanky to scrub off some of the red mud that coated it, I bit into its vast roundness, dawdling home chewing placidly for I loved raw vegetables. Cooked ones I could live without, thank you, particularly Aunty's soggy heaps of mashed something-or-other.

Of course I got told off for starting on it.

"Why couldn't you wait till you got home and I could cook it for supper properly, instead of eating in the lane as if you were starving. Look at you, red mud all round your face. Suppose somebody saw you?" Who? Us and Mrs A were the only ones in a half-mile stretch. No matter, I'd shown Aunty May up – although she was pleased to get a free vegetable, once I explained how Tom didn't understand when I told him. Chewed top cut off, the swede was boiled tasteless, mashed and served up for supper, quite ruined.

A distant rumbling cut across my daydreaming, coming from behind me, round the bend where I couldn't see unless I ran up to Aunty's bedroom. If it was Tom and the cart with Bobs or Charley, he was going the wrong way. Anyway whatever was coming along was far heavier and getting nearer.

Grinding up the steep slope, a strange high lorry came round the corner, filling the lane and almost touching the hedges either side. It was brown and had a big cream star painted on the side. It moved slowly past and I could see lots of men in pale brown uniforms, sitting all round in the open back. As I stared after them, another lorry came by, then another, then some small open cars, all filled with the same-looking men.

Seeing me on the gate they smiled and some of them waved. One called out in a strange voice, just like on the Pictures,

"Hi li'l gurl," and another said, "Ain't she cute?" and threw a little pack of green-paper sticks towards me. Feeling suddenly shy, not knowing what to do, I slid off the gate and stared through the wooden bars at them. I thought Aunty ought to know and turned to run and tell her. But she was already there, standing on the front path, watching.

"Yes, I saw, Louise; wait till they've all gone and then you can pick it up. Go back to the gate and wave to them, dear, that's right. They're waving at you, look!"

Well! Aunty must know who these people were if I could keep what they threw. This couldn't be the Enemy, who were supposed to drop sweets and chocolate from aeroplanes and if you ate any you'd die because they'd be poisoned. If you found something like that you were forbidden to pick it up but had to run and tell a grown-up. I never found anything and after a while forgot to look.

When the lane had been silent for a long time Aunty took a quick look up and down and said it was all right to go and collect my prize.

"What is it? And who are all those people? What are they doing in our lane?"

"They're American soldiers, helping us to win the War. They've been in other places but now they've come to Devon. And very welcome they are too, even though some people might say different, but don't you listen to them." Aunty seemed to be talking more to herself than me. I nudged her arm, holding up my pack of sticks under her nose. "That's chewing gum, Louise, don't open it now, save some for Santie, after tea.

"Ah, at last! I felt a spot of rain then, did you? Hope it doesn't start before Santie gets home or she'll be soaked. Perhaps Fred ought to take the big umbrella and meet her, I'll ask him.

"Just think," Aunty chattered on happily, "if you hadn't missed school today you wouldn't have seen the Americans – not that I like you getting these headaches. I wonder if I should get your eyes tested? Mmm, better have a word with Mummy first though, eh? Well! you'll have plenty to tell Santie when she comes in; that tongue of yours will wag nineteen to the dozen – make up for this morning, eh, poor old Pieface?"

Aunty May was on the right tack though it was some years later and Santie who made the discovery that I could hardly see the cinema across the London street, let alone read the name RAY MILLAND (my then favourite) in huge letters above the entrance. Advice was sought and glasses have been with me ever since – as have the headaches, but at least I can clearly see I'm taking the right tablets.

Chapter Thirteen

"You look hot and bothered, Pieface. Have you been running? Those geese haven't been chasing you again, have they?"

"Oh Aunty, DON'T! Don't remind me!" shuddering with remembered horror. "No, I walked, but I'm so HOT, Aunty. Can't I take my Liberty off?"

"We-e-ll I'm not sure," Aunty frowned. "It's a bit early in the year although it has turned very warm and you do seem overheated. If this weather keeps up I suppose it'll be all right. Yes, take it off – but put your sports coat on if you play outside!" Aunty called after me as I thundered joyfully up the stairs.

Santie and I hated our Liberty bodices. Worn over your vest (which was tucked into your knickers) these thick cotton garments had vertical reinforcing tapes stitched front and back and rubber buttons low down on each side, to hook suspenders on if you wore stockings as Santie did in the winter – brown woolly ones, probably knitted by Mum. Stockings were far too grown-up for me so Mum still had a regular customer for her thick long grey socks, forever sliding down so I had to stop all the time and pull them up. Aunty May tried threading elastic through the tops to keep them tidy but the painful red rim under my knees was worse than the wrinkled bunches below them, so she took it all out again.

"Wonder why they call them Liberty bodices? There's no liberty when you've got them on," grumbled Santie as we pulled them over our heads each morning, once the autumn set in. Dreadfully constricting at first, by the time the warmer weather came you were so used to your Unliberty that it felt strange when you finally left it off.

Freed at last, I flung the bodice on my bed and, frock half on again, burrowed in the woolly drawer for a cardigan, yet another product of Mum's busy needles, tossing the neatly folded jumpers aside like a dog burying a bone.

"Santie says at school sports coats are called 'cardigans'," I remarked, down in the kitchen once more, hanging off Aunty's arm with both hands and hopping on one foot, using her as a rail, chanting "CAR-DI-GAANS, CAR-DI-GAANS," with each hop.

"Don't do that dear, you'll pull me over and I don't care what they're called at school as long as you've put one on. Did you wash your hands when you were up there? No, I thought not. No, not over the SINK, can't you see the VEGETABLES in the bowl? I don't want soap on them, you chump. LOUISE! You don't have to run everywhere! You're like a cat with the wind in its tail today, what's the matter with you?"

For I had rushed away again, having heard a distant whistle's shriek and raced up the stairs, to crane out of our bedroom window. You couldn't see the actual train though because the culvert through which it ran was beyond Bobs and Charley's field and down a scrambly bank. But the smoke hung in the sky in a long line, marking the train's progress to Torquay and Brixham where Aunt Lucy, Uncle Fred's sister, lived with Uncle George. Aunty May's house, set among steep hills less than half a mile from The Halt where the main GWR line forked to run both behind and in front of the house, meant trains puffed and clanked all round us, pure heaven for me and Uncle Fred.

"Don't forget – WASH YOUR HANDS! Oh there you are, Santie, go and see what that imp's getting up to, there's a dear. She's racing about like I don't know what."

"What are you being so soppy for?" Santie came into the bedroom where I was still shouting 'CAR-DI-GAANS!' through the open window.

"Look!" pointing at the discarded bodice. "Aunty said I could take my Liberty bodice off, it's so hot. I'm sure you can too. D'you think she'll let us have a picnic tomorrow? Will you ask her, Sant, please? Plee-ee-ze?"

"I don't think she will." Santie was changing out of her posh school uniform, untwizzling suspenders, throwing off woolly stockings. "It's a bit early and she'll only say 'ne'er cast a clout till May be out,' whatever that's supposed to mean. She might let us go to Honeypots though, if they're open yet. You come past every day, Lou, did you notice?"

I shook my head. The people at Honeypots were always in evidence anyway and the door stood open all the time in nice weather so how could I tell?

"You're hopeless. They put a board out with O-P-E-N on it, ninny. You *can* read, I suppose?" Santie's sarcasm suddenly left her and she went a bit pink. "Oh, they're only open weekends now, aren't they, so the board wouldn't be out today, would it? Sorry, Lou – but you're still a ninny!" And she darted off to the bathroom with me in hot pursuit, to dibble our flannels in the cold water and splash it over each other.

Although there were hot and cold taps to the bath and washbasin, hot water came out of the kitchen tap only, heated by the range in the back room which, of necessity, was kept alight day and night, all year round. Fixed over the kitchen sink was a small black pump so every day Aunty pumped the handle up and down vigorously and the house clonked as water circulated through the pipes.

We had a cold 'lick and a promise' each morning and a 'proper hot wash' before bedtime, except Fridays, of course – Bath Night. You were only allowed five inches of hot water, yet another saving to help us win the War, and Uncle had painted a short green line one side of the bath to mark where five inches came to. Santie and I usually bathed at the same time, one either end facing, and when we got in the water it rose very high, way above Uncle's green line. So this five inches business was a complete mystery to me. Neither could I work out how the water went back to its mark when we got out, finally deciding Santie and me soaked it up in our skins, like our flannels did, getting squeezed out in the big fluffy towel.

"Aunty, can we go to Honeypots tomorrow if they're open? We could go down the lane in the morning to find out and go on to the Village to get any shopping you might want. Can we do that, Aunty please?" Santie was at her most wheedling, winsome. Who could refuse? The bit about the shopping was a brilliant touch. Good old Santie! Aunty May melted.

"If the weather stays the same then I don't see why not. It'll do us all good to get out in the fresh air and another garden to look at will make a nice change. I'll ask your Uncle if he'll come too. Louise, ask Gramps – yes I know he never comes with us," for I'd groaned, "Oh Aunty, why?"

"But you must ask him just to be polite, it's unkind not to. Be my good little girl, now. I'm sure Grandad will be pleased that you asked him anyway."

Honeypots Tea Gardens were at the far end of the lane, beyond which you turned to go over the railway bridge to school. They were open on summer weekends, weather permitting, tea being served at little iron tables in the orchard garden. There was a small paved area adjoining the house with a few extra tables, where you dashed with your tea things if it unexpectedly came on to rain. On a big old apple tree at the bottom of the garden, whose boundary fence bordered the railway cutting, hung a swing and no matter how hard I pushed I could never swing high enough above the trees to see the rushing trains below the steep bank.

Honeypots itself was a small thatched cottage set back from the lane down a sudden slope. Two middle-aged ladies ran the tea gardens, tended the small livestock and kept house for an older brother and their elderly mother, who baked all the cakes and bread for them.

These friendly, energetic women were charmingly old-fashioned, wearing their hair in coiled plaits over each ear, long skirts to their ankles and shiny black boots on rushing feet. They ran everywhere, skirts flying and boots twinkling down the lane. I loved them and was waved at each afternoon as I returned from school, through a window so low they had to stoop to see up to the lane. Sometimes I would be beckoned in and given two shiny buns or some rolls in a brown bag, warm from the oven, to take home for our tea.

Like Miss Crouch, you could feel the genuine warmth of their feelings towards us. No talking down to you or bright empty smiles, whatever your age you were part of their society. The Honeypots ladies were our friends.

By the side of the cottage along a narrow path by a deep stream was The Mill House, with mill race and fully working water wheel. Standing on the damp wooden platform, clinging tight to the safety rail to watch the wheel turning, deafened and exhilarated by the noise, the slapping as each paddle hit the water, throwing out fountains of spray as they came up and round and slapped down again. Inside the clanking mill house the stones turned, grinding into flour the corn supplied by local farmers.

The ladies' brother, Mr George, was in charge here. He hardly ever spoke though his welcoming smiles were warm. He never stopped us from watching the water wheel or standing in the dusty mill house, although we must have got under his feet sometimes. He kept his eyes on us all the time though, moving us back if we got too close to the rushing water or heavy grindstones.

Mr George seemed to work alone for I rarely saw anyone else there. We only went to Honeypots at weekends though so perhaps he had help during the week. When you did hear voices coming from the mill and the gate at the cottage end of the path was locked, it meant Mr George was extra busy and we couldn't disturb him.

The really horrible thing about Honeypots was THE GEESE who, like the pigs, were the bane of my life. As well as ducks and chickens, rabbits and bees, the ladies kept a gaggle of large grey geese, pink of foot and angry-eyed, either watchfully quiet or loudly honking.

Except if the tea gardens were open, when they were safely locked in their little house and wire-fenced away from the visitors, these nasty-tempered birds could be seen swimming on the Village Pond close by. This pond was really just a wider bit of the tiny stream that ducked under the low bridge by the Church. Coloured pebbles glinted and twinkled under the fast-running, crystal-clear water. It was quite shallow and Santie told me that one hot afternoon she had bent down to scoop up and drink it.

"It was icy-cold," she said, "and tasted really lovely, sort of bubbly, you know." I didn't nor did I ever try, because I was too small to bend over the low bridge, terrified I'd fall in and drown, or be eaten by the horrible geese.

By the time I came home from school they were in the field above the pond, grazing along its edge or sitting preening, oiling their feathers, and could be safely ignored for they never left the field until fetched home. Still, every day my footsteps slowed as I turned the corner into the lane, looking fearfully towards the pond, for if they were on the water they set up a loud honking or flapped their great wings.

One dreadful afternoon I rounded the corner and there, standing in the lane, were four geese. The others idly swam round and round on the water behind them. I stopped dead, fear pricking me all over and glanced desperately up and down the lane. Not a soul in sight. Staring at the strangely silent geese as though hypnotised, I told myself I must walk past them or I'd never get home. I thought if I tiptoed by they mightn't see me.

Keeping so close to the hedge that it scratched my arm, I started edging along, never taking my eyes off the geese for an instant. Just as I drew level the four in the lane ran forward honking, wings extended and the ones in the water rose up as one and came after them. I fled, screaming,

"THE GEESE ARE CHASING ME! THE GEESE ARE CHASING ME!" pursued by the hissing spiteful birds, necks extended inches behind my bare legs.

The ladies were running towards me, one catching me up, the other shouting, waving her arms, kicking in among the geese, driving them back towards the pond. Carried crying into the cottage, hugged close, kissing my wet and frightened face, Miss Margaret sat down, rocking and soothing me till my sobs subsided into hiccups.

"Those blamed birds, I'll wring all their necks before I'm done, frightening dear little Louise like that!" Miss Alice came panting into the kitchen where I was being comforted.

"I'll just telephone to Mrs Sherwood, tell her you'll be a bit late, and then us'll walk up home with you, shan't we, Mother?"

Mother nodded, beaming, putting a plate with a currant cake on it in front of me, pouring milk into a beaker, kissing my cheek as she passed.

By the time I'd finished my impromptu tea, Aunty May arrived and I burst into fresh howls while she there-there'd and tutted, clutching me to her friendly front. Over my head I heard snatches of conversation.

"All my fault, Mrs Sherwood, I was just coming to fetch them when I heard her screaming, poor little mite. It'll never happen again, I'll make sure they're all in the shed before the school comes out in future, I promise. Really spiteful they can be sometimes, geese. They tried a peck or two at Mother once and she soon give 'em what-for, didn't she, Marg?"

"You have to be firm, show them who's boss," Miss Alice continued. "If only Louise had faced them and shouted, waved her arms, they'd have been as good as gold. She says she tried to tippy-toe by, so they thought she was creeping up to catch them – that's why they give chase like that, seeing her off. They're quite brainy for birds, is geese."

"Yes, I see, Alice," Aunty May, arm round my shoulders, was moving towards the open door. "Luckily there's no real harm done. She's just had a nasty fright, haven't you Lou? But if you could make sure they're not in the lane when she comes along I'd be grateful. I'll take her home now; Santie will be wondering what's happened though I told Mr Sherwood but you know how he forgets sometimes. Oh, how kind you are, thank you, yes we will enjoy them."

For a warm brown bag had been pressed into Aunty's hand as she steered me up the path and on to the lane, the little group in the tiny doorway waving till we turned the corner.

"What an adventure, eh Pieface? The ladies say you were very brave and only cried a little bit. I've never liked geese myself, nasty noisy things making enough row to wake the dead. Still it scares off intruders or foxes, so they're some use after all. Look, there's Santie at the gate, waiting for us. You can tell her all about it after supper but then try and put it out of your mind. The geese won't bother you any more."

Nor did they, for from that day on Miss Alice made sure not a goose was in sight when I came along. But I never ever forgot the fright I got and even today, watching Canada geese tamely and quietly minding their own business in Kew Gardens, a faint shudder of memory will come over me, if I let it.

Chapter Fourteen

PLONG-G-G, PLONK, plink-plong-plink, PLOL-LOL-LON-G-G, pling! What a row, coming from the drawing room. Aunty May was hovering at the foot of the stairs as I came jumpy-jump down, one step at a time, on a sunny morning.

"The Piano Tuner is here, Louise, now don't you go bothering him. You can watch from the doorway but stay out of his way." Then, turning to a tall thin man sitting on the piano stool, "if you just call me when you've finished I'll come and fetch you."

A warning frown at me followed. Aunty knew there was not a hope of even *trying* to keep me away from the drawing room when something exciting was going on, so with a further shake of her head she went off down the hall, leaving me 'on trust'. The thunderous jangling notes rolled round the house and for a while I stood curiously in the doorway, like a good girl. But I wanted to see what the tuner was actually doing as he stretched across the piano, his right hand twiddling with a black fork among the strings in the back, while his left hand pressed down the keys one at a time.

I started creeping silently towards him and was halfway across the room when he said to the piano,

"Hallo, little one. You can come and stand by me if you want to, you won't be in my way."

How did he know I was there? For his white stick lay across the settee and he wore dark glasses even indoors. I stood under his left elbow, watching closely, breathing damply on his hand in my eagerness to peer round him at the unseen fork. The piano took up nearly all one end of the small room, almost into the wide bay window where a large settee filled what little space remained. It seemed rude to squash round him for a better view, more so because he was blind.

Realising I'd have to stay put, now seemed a good time to try out the conversational skills I was secretly copying by carefully watching Aunty and her friends. A good mimic with a quick ear, I soon could do a passable imitation and had their light tinkly laughs off to a T. Once without thinking I used Mrs Benson's distinctive high voice, gasping,

"Oh my dear soul!" at one of Santie's tales, who rocked with laughter, squeaking,

"That's just *her*, Lou, how clever!"

So far I had only practised with Teddy, in the White House. Deep breath and...

"How do you do? So nice to meet you. Yes, it is, isn't it? Are you left-handed? I am. So's my sister. And my Mummy, except when she writes." Pause. "Yes, that's right. I can play Chopsticks with BOTH hands though. Can you? What does tuner mean? Did you come on the bus?" Pause again. "Yes, it is a long walk, I agree. What's that little fork for? Why can't you see? How did you know I was there? I kept ever so quiet."

The piano tuner didn't give the rehearsed answers, in fact didn't speak at all. He just smiled into the piano, continuing to dong a finger heavily on one key. I had forgotten he wasn't Teddy, who always kept the conversation going, replying in the proper places. After a minute or so, running out of steam I faltered to a stop.

"I see with my ears," he said at last, turning to face me. "I knew you were there perhaps even before you came down the stairs. Come round this side, you can't see the strings from where you are." So I squashed round, excuse-me'ing and kicking the piano stool which was pulled much further out than usual. "I listen to the note and if it's not true, then I use this fork, as you call it, to tighten or loosen the string, to get a perfect pitch. Would you like to help? Push down one of the keys, any one will do."

Really? He wanted *me* to help him? All the misery of my conversational failure flew out the window as delightedly I DONG-DONG'd while the piano tuner explained patiently about hammers and vibrations, loud and soft pedals, and what the strings did when you pressed each key but as usual I wasn't listening properly. Hardly heard a word in fact for, given the chance to 'play' the piano, I plonked up and down quickly, before Aunty called out,

"Stop that awful noise, Louise, for pity's sake," like she always did if I found the lid up after she'd been dusting, for the rows of black-and-white teeth were like a magnet to little fingers.

I moved back a fraction, knocking his elbow, bumping against the settee but the piano tuner didn't seem to notice. He just played some loud chords, fingers flashing up and down and then, grinning broadly, played Chopsticks so fast that his hands went blurry.

"I've finished now, Louise, let's go and find Mrs Sherwood, shall we?" He closed the lid and stood up, the tallest man I'd ever seen, his head almost touching the blue-painted glass shade shaped like a bluebird with half-closed wings, which hung from the ceiling. Sliding his hand over the side of the settee the piano tuner picked up his stick, hat and coat and made briskly for the hall, pausing in the doorway, smiling face turned back to where I stood open-mouthed. I followed him into the back room and he called,

"Here we are, Mrs Sherwood, all finished, thank you. That piano keeps in pretty good condition considering it doesn't get a lot of use these days. When are you going to start the children on it? Louise seems quite keen already."

I left them talking and wandered back towards the drawing room as it was ages since I'd had a good snoop in it. I might even peek in the dining room opposite, though that was my least favourite room in the house; still, there might be something of interest, you never knew. It was very quiet, I could hear a wasp buzzing against the window in the porch room through the closed glass-panelled door, the only sound really except for the clocks, just starting to strike half-past ten.

Aunty's house was full of clocks, two or more in nearly every room, even an old one on the window sill in the Outside. The whole house ticked softly all the time, like gentle breathing, and reverberated loudly every half-hour, for most of them chimed. So you got a prolonged peal, the old Grandfather clock outside our bedroom door starting its wheezing clank first, like a signal for the others who followed, echoing round for five minutes or more. It was Uncle Fred's daily task to wind up the clocks and this he did unfailingly every night, moving slowly from room to room. Occasionally a man came out from Exeter to look at them, going round with Uncle Fred, and no clock escaped his notice.

Aunty May called him The Regulator and when I asked why, she said well, that's what he was of course. Daddy, when applied to, twinkled at me, saying it was because he came to the house regularly and although Mum said,

"Oh Jim! Don't confuse the child," it made perfect sense to me.

Unless waiting for a particular time to strike, or trying to eavesdrop on private conversations, I never noticed the clocks. Like the pipes clonking or the wireless chattering, they were the daily creaks and door slams of the house. Part of your life, like your heart thumping after running upstairs, or if something frightened you.

"Don't yer Anty 'ave a lot o'clocks, Louise! I never seen so many at once. What they all for?" Rose said to my intense surprise, on a rare occasion when she actually came in with me after playing out. They must have been striking, though I didn't notice for, apart from playground gossip when *everyone* went through it, Rose never asked directly or commented about anything to do with Aunty May. She was a little afraid of her, daunted by Aunty's apparent grand manner and big house. Not that it made a scrap of difference to our close friendship, staunch and stubborn the both of us.

Eventually, when more than one silly grown-up cried in mock alarm,

"Goodness me! What a dreadful noise! I can hardly hear myself think with all that going on!" it dawned on me that a house with so many clocks was unusual, especially when the visitor put their hands over their ears as well.

Mrs Bennett, Aunty's friend we didn't like much, did that but only the once for Santie put on her sweetest face and said,

"What clocks? What clocks is that, Mrs Bennett? I can't hear anything – can you, Louise?" She turned innocently to me behind her and just an eyelid flutter told me what was going on.

"NO, SANTIE, I CAN'T HEAR ANYTHING AT ALL!" I yelled and twitched mightily. Mrs Bennett got flustered, laughing nervously. Auntie just *looked* at Santie, hurrying us away but not before I spotted that lovely squiggly turn of her mouth and knew we hadn't really let her down. Mrs Bennett's "Goodness me!" and ear-clapping also went into my mimic's hat, to be honed and polished, ready for the next 'show'.

As well as the cuckoo clock in the back room there was another in the kitchen but it had lost part of its bellows and only went 'Dong! COOK!' each half-hour, which Aunty said was very suitable for a kitchen clock. On the wall above Aunty's work-table was a frying-pan clock, but it didn't go properly. Santie said it was electric, so I suppose it had to be turned off, like Aunty's cooker.

Out in the hall hung two curved and (Uncle said) empty sword-cases with above them a large black-cased clock which although it didn't strike, had a loud and sonorous tick, black hands jerking round its clear white face. Like my favourite on the landing, this clock had funny figures too, all V's and X's and III's, which I didn't understand, though able to tell the time quite easily. Another of life's mysteries never explained properly for when I pointed at VII and asked what it meant, Santie said,

"It's quarter to seven, what's the matter with you?"

All the bedrooms had a small alarm on the bedside table, but as we had no space in our tiny room our clock stood on the chest of drawers, green to match the mirror, brush and comb set. In the spare room on the mantelpiece there was a gold clock too, with little balls that twirled round and round, which I found endlessly fascinating. A shiny clock with two big bells on the top stood on the shelf in the bathroom; Santie fiddled with it one afternoon and the resultant PING-G-G-ING!! was so loud she dropped it on the floor in fright. It still worked though, back on its shelf, ticking our bath-time away over the years.

So it was no surprise to find three clocks in the drawing room. A black one with a gold face ponderously chimed each hour from its home on the mantelpiece. A white china clock painted with tiny blue flowers sat on a side table and one of two 'Grandmothers' stood against the wall between the piano and the fireplace. Its twin was in the dining room opposite and they Westminster chimed in concert with one another.

The blue-and-white drawing room was stuffed to bursting point with furniture and pieces of china so you had to move very carefully not to bump yourself or worse, knock over a table lamp or send a favourite piece flying. Considering the way Santie and I tore about and Aunty May's bulk weaving delicately among the tables and chairs, accidents were few.

Surprisingly, Aunty May was never ever cross if anything in the house got broken. Little everyday annoyances really irritated her but something smashed or a huge spreading stain on the carpet was just cleared up with a mild,

"Never mind, dear, you couldn't help it."

It was nothing to do with my 'shakes' either; be it Uncle, Gramps or Santie – even Ginger – she never grumbled or accused. After first making sure nobody was hurt, she just quietly got rid of the mess.

A large, polished wooden box with a handle at the side stood under the window. When you opened the hinged lid, which had a picture of roses painted on its inside, there was a metal cylinder with millions of pins sticking out in a pattern all over. Aunty would loop a fat roll of paper with holes in, on to the cylinder, give a quick turn or two on the handle to start the metal tube revolving. As the paper roll turned with it, unwinding slowly, a little tune tinkled out.

Aunty said the music box was very old and fragile so it was rarely heard. Watching the pins pricking the paper on the turning cylinder was the best part, for I was unimpressed by the thin 'music' it produced, preferring the jolly bands on Aunty's wireless. I could dance about to them and joined in loudly when I knew the tunes, making up the words as I went along. Not that there was any room to move, let alone dance, in Aunty's overstuffed parlour.

I had just finished snuffling about, pleased to find everything exactly the same as the last time I looked, when the back room door suddenly opened. Although not doing anything wrong, I am in my private world, thinking my own thoughts, will be tetchy if disturbed. So I dart quickly across into the dining room, standing behind the half-closed door as Gramps comes along the hall, turns and goes slowly up the stairs.

I am now in a very long room, running the length of the house, front bay windows matching those of the drawing room on the right of the front door. This is 'the best room' and used only on rare occasions – like Christmas, when Uncle Fred carries the heavy wireless in and we sit eating the Christmas cake Aunty May has made according to the special Wartime recipe in *Woman's Weekly*, listening to whatever catches her fancy as she twiddles round the dial.

Although called the dining room, we don't use it as such. Visitors come regularly only to tea, they never 'dine' with us. A big oak table was pushed against the end wall, matching chairs tucked all round it, so perhaps guests had dined here once upon a time, before Wartime austerity put an end to dinner-parties.

A china cabinet, whose glass-fronted doors rattled every time I dashed past, and a bureau stood against the walls, settee and armchairs grouped round the fireplace. The only really pretty thing in the room was the painted glass ceiling light, made in the shape of a large yellow butterfly, its open wings tipped with orange. Like the bluebird light, the fitting for the bulb was hidden among the wings, a fiddly job to change when it 'popped', so neither light was switched on much, a standard lamp being put on instead.

Too dim to be of much use, the lamp cast its orange glow on the 'owl' clock on the wall above, whose eyes moved, tick-left, tock-right, with every swing of its pendulum. I imitated this too, to Santie's delight, as one of my party pieces. Thankfully the clock was silent so I didn't have to go "t'wit t'woo" as well.

Even on a brilliant summer day the light from the big windows wasn't enough to reach the furthest corners of the room. There was a smaller window at one side but this was slightly obscured by the woodpile, that infamous stack of poles and branches where I learnt what happens when you tamper with birds' eggs, which leaned against the wall outside. On windy winter nights loose twigs sometimes tapped on the window, frightening the life out of me if the door was open as I passed on my way to bed, sending me flying up the stairs away before whatever new terror it was could get me.

Mum reckoned the dining room was damp.

"Stands to reason, Jim," she said, when we were all together one weekend and she thought little ears weren't listening, drawn up to the table in the back room doing a nice new jigsaw, my favourite indoor pastime, which she and Dad had brought down for me. "Keeping a stack of wood against a brick wall is bound to let a bit of damp in, specially in an old house like this."

Daddy nodded, said the damp-course had probably gone anyway, and he thought it was the same in the drawing room, if he wasn't mistaken.

I didn't like sitting in the dining room, even when we were all there together. I was scared of the shadows, especially in the corners where Trolls might be lurking, although Aunty said "of course there aren't, don't be silly, trolls is it now? Whatever next?" But they *did* live in the fields, it said so in my Big Book of Fairy Stories, and they marched along in the deep muddy ruts left by carts. If you crouched down low you just might see the green feather in their hats bobbing along, the only bit of a troll that was visible above ground. I never dared to look, more because of the rucking I'd get from Aunty May for lying on a wet field than the terrifying thrill of actually seeing trolls' hats.

"I'm going to stay up ALL NIGHT," I announced one Christmas afternoon, perched on a dumpty (Aunty's name for footstools) by the fire, as far away from the troll-hiding corners as possible, waiting for The King to speak to us, as if by magic, on Aunty's wireless.

"Of course you are, Pieface, and Santie too, as it's her birthday. We'll all stay up till Boxing Day."

"You'll fall asleep, I bet you" Santie said scornfully. "Won't she, Aunty? We'll stay awake though, won't we?"

Late that evening, completely worn out I struggled to keep my eyes open, stubbornly determined to prove Santie wrong.

Flopped on the settee, fingering the fluffy pink ears of my new brown Christmas rabbit, I heard the clock on the mantelpiece, its top pointed like a church steeple, striking and sleepily counted the strokes.

"Wake up, Lou," Aunty May was bending over me, "look, it's nearly nine o'clock! It'll soon be morning, so why don't you let Santie take you up to bed for a little while, or you'll be too tired to eat any breakfast. Give me a kiss and I'll come and tuck you in, there's a good girl," as I sat up, "in a few minutes."

Wanting to stay, too tired to protest, snuggled under my eiderdown at last, I remembered that the clock had indeed struck nine times. Nine o'clock was so far past my bedtime, so very late, that I knew I'd been up all night after all.

Voices in the hall bring me hurrying out of my daydream. Aunty is calling over her shoulder, "Not at all, it won't take me a moment" and she picks up the phone, dials and pauses. Then, "Hello Maud dear, it's May. Mr Clark is on his way, just leaving us now." Aunty is using her Front Door voice, which suddenly swoops upwards, "Oh really? How very kind! You can catch him before he leaves? Are you sure? Then I'll ask him to wait. Goodbye till Wednesday, that's right, me to you, usual time. Bye!"

This sounds promising so I hurry to catch Aunty before she returns to the back room, trying to clutch my short arms round her ample middle. Aunty shrieks, "AG -H! Oh Louise, you made me jump! Where did you spring from? You should be out in the fresh air, a lovely day like this, not mooning about the house. Get along with you!"

The piano tuner (presumably Mr Clark) is talking quietly in the conservatory with Uncle Fred, their voices mingling softly, each man a native of the area. Fingers edging the slatted shelf, Mr Clark taps a pot, runs his hand delicately over the plant and they murmur on together, to the next one.

Aunty and I join them, although I am shooed out the door to play in the sunshine. As the door remains open and Aunty has important things to tell Mr Clark, I duck down against the wall to listen so as not to miss anything worth reporting to Santie – where is she, by the way, haven't seen her all morning.

"Here's a piece of luck!" Aunty says brightly, "Mr Crouch has just taken the car over to Milber to fetch their cousin – in plaster, poor thing, broke her ankle – so Mr Crouch feels it's all right to use his petrol ration as she can't get on the bus. As he's got the car anyway Miss Crouch is ringing them now to tell him to stop here on the way back and collect you. He'll be about twenty minutes she thinks, I said you'd wait. Well, it'll save you that long walk up past the Village. No really, NO TROUBLE AT ALL," Aunty raises her voice, drowning Mr Clark's protest. "There's plenty of room for you both and Mrs

Stout's crutches – it's all sorted out. So now, would you like another cup of tea, Mr Clark?"

Chapter Fifteen

For some time now, although nothing had been actually said, even the dullest children were becoming aware that something Special was being planned, involving the whole school – yes, even the Big Ones in their classrooms up Constitution Hill. Mr Marsh, Mr Nichols and Miss Lucas had been spotted several times in the School Hall talking earnestly with Mrs Moffatt and dear Miss Digby. They were always there for Assembly every morning of course, for 'Glad That I Live Am I' or 'All Things Bright and Beautiful' and another story about Jesus before "And now, children, all stand for The Blessing". To be all together on several afternoons, long after we'd gone home, was a cause for great speculation.

Playtimes were rife with gossip and rumours flew about, as we stood in little groups in the thin sunshine, eating our 'snails', lovely sticky buns the kind baker at the top of the Village sent down to the school as a treat on really cold winter mornings.

"What's goin' on then? Do 'e know waat tis?"

"Doan' arst I", Jessie Collins spoke thickly, through a mouthful of dough. "Arst me bruther in Old Nick's class but he knows nuffin, *so 'e zes*", she added darkly.

Lily the Vaccee comes running out of the lavs, waving, shouting across the playground before puffing up to us.

"I got sumthin' to tell yah, wait till I gits me bref back".

We crowd round, Rose and I busy unwinding our snail coils, turning them inside out, squashing the bun into a big round ball, from which we pick off tiny bits to make it last longer.

Lily begins,

"Oo's got me bun? Ta, Pammy. 'Ere, you know I told yah yesterdee about Mrs T, lives next door to us, Eileen's that is – YES I DID!" she shouts, for some of us are shaking our heads in puzzlement. "Well, I'll tell yah agin, just this once, so LISTEN! You know she cleans the classrooms an' that arter school, well yesterdee they was all there agin, all the teechus. Got the music books aht, she said, and Ma Lucas starts thumpin' on the pianner fit to bust. AND I KNOW WOT'S HAPPENIN, SO THERE!"

She stops, triumphant, gazing round at her goggling audience.

"'Ow d'yer find out? 'oo told yer? 'oo zed? 'Ginger' Beer challenges, picking the very few currants out of his bun and chucking them at a surprised starling.

"*I* SEZ, YOU GOT CLOFF EARS?" Lily, inflamed by this Doubting Thomas, pushes at the middle of Ginger's coat; startled, he drops his bun. "Now look wot you dun – 'waste not, want not', you'll cop it", she crows as he bends to pick it up and placidly resumes currant-picking. "Don't frow them currants about, gi'm 'ere, I'll eat 'em. *I* KNOW", she continues importantly, "cos I 'eard 'er, Mrs T, telling Eily's Ma meself, didn' I? 'I see they'm goin' to 'ave A PADGIT dahn the school, that'll take some doin' an no mistake' she says over the 'edge – didn't see me and Eiley coming dahn from the Village be'ind 'er, we 'eard every word".

"Where's Eileen anyway? Ain't seen 'er today". Jessie sprays a few crumbs at Lily through the gap where her front teeth were two days before.

"Gawd, be careful, mind me new mac – 'ow much yer get for them old teef of yourn, Jess? Worf a packet, them. She's got a cold, ain't she, Eil, not coming today, nor tomorrer. So, A PADGIT! Wot d'ya fink of *that*, you lot?"

Lily spins round on one foot then, having picked all the currants out of Ginger's bun and eaten them, proceeds to eat the bun as well. Ginger, like all of us slightly intimidated by Lily, opens his mouth to protest, thinks better of it and just watches her in dismay.

A Padgit? What's a Padgit when it's at home? Nobody knows. Neither it seems does Lily for when I timidly ask her she turns on me shouting,

"Ow the 'ell do I know? I jus' sed I knew wot it *was*, not what it *meant*. Still I 'spect us'll find aht sooner or la'er when they feels like tellin' us" and she whirlwinds away, carrying her news to another huddled group – though everybody has heard her already, probably did in Newton too, for Lily's is the loudest voice in the school.

After a pause Derek Hobbs, the quiet one in our class, speaks slowly and thoughtfully to his toecap scuffing on the ground,

"If her zes the teachers is practisin' singin' then it aren't someone cummin' to see us, like a cunjerurr, or tekking us on A Outin' to The Pandymime or somethin'. A Padgit must be like what we 'ad at Christmas and our Mums cum and we had to do all the work, larnin' lines an' dressing up. Thaat's what I think anyway," and he looks up at our amazed and silent faces for this is quite the longest speech Derek has ever made.

Nobody has anything else to offer so, nodding in agreement, the group breaks up and we go and line up two-by-two by the main door, for Mrs Moffatt, having attempted to get us to,

"Run about, children, come on, get some exercise, you'll soon warm up, don't just stand about shivering," has given up and blown the Going-In whistle five minutes early.

Please God not the pantomime, I pray. Aunty May took Santie and me to Torquay in the Christmas holidays to see it and after counting the days in excited anticipation the actual experience was a huge letdown. I didn't like any of it, not one little bit.

Despite being provided with a small paper cone of sweets which a smiling lady in uniform handed to each child as we came in, I became fidgety and fretful before very long, twisting round in my seat, standing up, kicking the seat in front, yawning, whining,

"I'm too hot, I'm tired, when are we going home?" every few minutes. Aunty had a quick consultation with Santie, who turned round and pointed out some spare seats next to Josie, a girl she knew at swimming classes. Aunty went up the aisle to speak to Josie's mother, placed Santie in her willing charge and took me out at last, away from the noise and confusion, to run gladly along the front in the cold fresh air. We went back to get Santie later, who seemed to have enjoyed herself immensely, said she'd had a really lovely time and was sorry when the pantomime ended.

On the bus going home, Aunty told Santie she wasn't surprised I hadn't liked it; it was far too old for me and why they put in things for grown-ups when it was all supposed to be for little children was beyond her.

"I only took you both because Clarkson Rose was in it and you know how famous he is. I naturally thought it would be suitable for Louise as well. Didn't you even like the Fairy Ballet, Pieface?" Her concerned face met my upturned one from where I was sprawled on her lap. "No? Never mind, we'll go again another year, when you're a big girl. Still, you got some nice sweets given you, didn't you?"

Famous or not, I particularly disliked, in fact was rather frightened by, the man with the red and white striped stockings in old-fashioned bunched-up skirts, who bumped about the stage with his bottom stuck out, sometimes showing spotted bloomers, and someone I couldn't see went BANG TISH! BANG TISH! on a drum as he did so. When he went away, people in dressing-up clothes stood on the stage calling out to us and you were meant to shout back. I couldn't though as I'd never been allowed to speak loudly anywhere other than at home or in school, let alone shout at actors on a stage. It wasn't my first visit to a theatre by any means; I enjoyed watching people dancing and singing, could follow a simple story to its Happy Ending. But this pantomime had no proper story at all, everything was confused and too loud and dazzling. They hadn't turned the lights off after we sat down either and this, added to the glittering stage, hurt my eyes, making me squint.

It wasn't a patch on the Pictures, that calm and cosy dark nest, where the lights went out as soon as the curtains rattled open and nobody asked you to shout things at them. Perched on the top of my tip-up seat at first for the best view, legs dangling, totally absorbed by the films. Then later cuddled on Aunty's lap, eyes still fixed on the screen though half-asleep. Nothing else in the whole world was as wonderful as going to the Pictures.

The morning sunshine has given in to a cold afternoon and the sky looks full of snow. Mrs Moffatt pulls the chain on the side of the four lamps that hang down the middle of the classroom and the gas jets plop and flicker before settling into a soft hiss. Mrs Moffatt is reading to us and we follow her in our books, pointing finger underlining each word. Suddenly she stops, looks up and glancing out the window says,

"Now, boys and girls, I'm sending you home earlier today as I don't like the look of that sky. But before you go I have something Very Important to tell you. So close your books, put them away – stop banging those lids, please! Sit up straight, hands in laps, that's right, and listen carefully to what I'm going to say." Whilst speaking Mrs Moffatt has crossed to the windows and dragged the blackout curtains across, tucking them round at the sides to prevent even the tiniest chink of pale light showing. Then she glances at her watch and comes to stand in front of us, waiting. Rose and I nudge each other: is this going to be IT? The Big News at last?

"Miss Lucas (the Headmistress) and all the teachers feel we ought to do something to cheer us all up; that means everybody, not just the school – the Village, your mummies and…" Her eyes flick to me and Lily and Peter Whatsit at the back,"…er… those grown-ups some of you are staying with at present. In fact all the people who look after you. So we had a little meeting and Miss Lucas decided that at the end of *next* term the school will put on a PAGEANT and your mummies..." she pauses again, resumes "...families will be invited, can take part if they wish."

Lily across the aisle turns to smirk a jubilant 'told yer so' round the class. "Face the front Lily, please, don't fidget. Pay attention to me, all of you, settle down. I don't want anybody coming to me later on saying they don't understand."

There is some scuffling and whispering behind me and, turning round, I see Tony Hodges being urged to put up a reluctant hand.

"YES Anthony, what IS it?" Mrs Moffatt represses a tut; we hold our breath.

"Please Miss, wot's a Padgit?"

"PAGEANT, Anthony, P-A-G-E-A-N-T." She steps up to the blackboard and prints in large letters, chalk squeaking loudly in the pin-drop silence of the classroom. "Repeat it after me all of you, PAGEANT" and we all chorus: "PADG-ET".

Sighing, Mrs Moffatt continues:

"Four weeks from now we break up for the Easter holidays. When you return parts will be given out and rehearsals will take place during the last two periods each Friday afternoon. The Pageant – which is a musical play by the way, children, with lots of short scenes so that all of you get a chance to be in it – those who want to, that is. These scenes will be very easy to learn and practice at home. The Pageant will be performed on the Saturday afternoon before we break up on the following Tuesday, so that grown-ups and your older sisters and brothers, those that have them, can come too."

Mrs Moffatt pauses, looking along the rows of rapt faces, eyes fixed on her, mouths open. A small buzz of whispers begins, growing louder, so she quickly continues, raising her voice slightly and the whispers stop instantly.

"The Pageant will be held in Constitution Hall as it's much bigger than the School Hall and we can fit a lot more people in. Those children with speaking parts must be word-perfect by the

Friday, when the final full rehearsal will be held and I know *my* girls and boys won't let THE SCHOOL down. You'll all do your very best, won't you?"

"OH YES MRS MOFFATT!" we chorus fervently.

"Good! I can see you're looking forward to the Pageant already, just as Miss Lucas and all of us are. One more thing before you go – we'd like some grown-up help too tell your parents, perhaps they could lend us a few things for some of our scenes, or help with costumes? Anyway we'll be asking all your mummies and aunties to a Parents' Meeting before we break up for Easter. Oh and make sure to tell them that none of you will be kept in after school; rehearsals will be held in School-time only."

This last remark was really addressed to those boys who ran errands and generally helped out on their fathers' farms, making it difficult for them to stay after Home-time. In fact, come Harvest when the whole family and neighbours pitched in, these boys sometimes didn't come to school for a week. The teachers knew this, it was reluctantly accepted, for with men away at the War the farmers needed all the help they could get.

Santie and I did our little bit too after school – not on the farms but at fruit-picking time; we particularly enjoyed helping in Mr Murray's orchard across the lane, opposite Mrs A's. Our job was to pick up fallen cider apples, checking there were no specks or bruises before putting them carefully into your very own little basket. When these were full the bigger boys tipped our contributions into huge baskets, nearly as tall as me. There was only one Very Important Rule and if you broke it you were sent home instantly, never to return. It was absolutely forbidden to rush about because of the ever-present danger of causing a nasty accident by wobbling the ladders propped against the trees on which grown-ups balanced, picking from the highest branches. You had to look behind you too before bending down for even a very small child bumping a ladder was enough to set it sliding.

Santie and I, mindful of the Rule, nevertheless were quick and efficient sorters, praised and held up as models to the other children. Not a bruise or dent escaped our gimlet eyes but then, sorting apples came naturally to us – most of those windfalls stored in the White House were collected by us. I loved being in the orchard, loved the sweet scents and the strong taste of the apples, for although you were supposed to put specky ones in a separate box not leave them on the ground for the birds to peck and get merry on, Uncle said, not a few found their way into my mouth or were stored in my apron pockets for nibbling later. I never associated the headachy feeling I sometimes had after apple-picking with the fruit; I just loved any old apples, and ate as many as I could get.

Mrs Moffatt glances at her watch and towards the darkening window again, is just saying,

"That's all for the moment, children and as some of you have quite a long walk home, we'll..." when the door behind us opens and she cries brightly "yes, Miss Lucas, we're just being Dismissed. Children! MISS LUCAS!"

We scramble to our feet, chorusing,

"Good afternoon, Miss Lucas" who replies softly, calmly coming in and holding the door open for us to file out, two by two, starting from the back. She says "go straight home" to each of us as we pass her, adding our name, and no child is left out. Miss Lucas loves children; if any of us run past when she is with someone in the Hall she calls you and, though continuing to talk to the teacher or visitor, draws you against her long skirts, resting her hand lightly on your head for a second, before sending you gently on your way.

As Rose and I sit in the second row furthest from the door we are almost the last to leave and I hear Mrs Moffatt, now standing next to Miss Lucas, murmur,

"Look at that sky! Getting darker by the minute. So much for Daylight Saving!"

Pixie-hoods tied on, coats buttoned up to our chins, we rush screaming across the playground and squash through the gates. No loitering about with Rose today; she sets off up Constitution Hill and I start running towards the bridge, not even glancing to see if the Italians are working on the railway line. One or two big flakes of snow float slowly down and as I get over the bridge I see Uncle Fred coming to meet me, carrying an umbrella, along the lane by the Pond and rush joyfully at him, shouting,

"WE'RE GOING TO HAVE A PADGET IN SCHOOL AND I'M IN IT WILL YOU COME?" up at his dear, smiling face.

St Mary's School Pageant became the most talked-about item at school and when the summer term started and preparations got under way, local excitement and interest grew. Not just in school either for Reverend Dyer announced during the Notices at Easter Sunday Service that "help with making and painting scenery is urgently needed so anyone who can give a little of their precious time please speak to Mr Marsh. The Ladies Tuesday Sewing Bee are already cutting patterns for costumes and would welcome spare materials or other assistance – please see Mrs Benson afterwards, thank you".

There was to be a lot of singing and some in my class, particularly those who were choirboys anyway, were involved in that, including me, and there were new songs to be learnt. I enjoyed singing so was happy for a while; but when individual acting parts began being given out I sat up hopefully, longing to be chosen. Although often shy meeting new people face-to-face, I had no qualms about singing or reciting to an audience – relishing the applause and chuckles that invariably followed my performances.

Soon most of the class had something extra to learn except me and as available parts dwindled so did my spirits; I'd been overlooked – ME – who wanted an individual piece to do so very much. Well, let them keep their silly old padget, see if *I* care. So I pretend indifference, telling nobody of the anguish I really feel.

Late one afternoon during the second week of the summer term, on my way from the lavatory block tucked away in a corner of the playground ("it's urgent, please Miss"), I was amazed to see Aunty May in the Hall talking earnestly to Miss Lucas.

"Hello Louise, just the young lady I was about to come and look for," beamed Miss Lucas. "Your Aunty and I have finished our little chat and as it's not far off Home-time I expect you'd like to take Louise now, wouldn't you Mrs Sherwood? Go and fetch your satchel, Louise, and don't forget your gas mask."

"Why have you come to fetch me, Aunty? Have I done something wrong?" Puzzled and anxious, I am being hurried along – no dawdling home today, that's for sure.

"No, Pieface, of course you haven't, why ever should you think that? You funny little thing", she twitches my hand about in hers, smiling down lovingly. "Miss Lucas wanted a word with me about you, something *nice*, and as I was down at the Guild today anyway it only took a moment to come over the bridge. No, I won't tell you now", she says as I start to speak, "I'll leave that to Mrs Moffatt; you'll find out soon enough."

Rushing home from school the very next afternoon, I burst into the back room shouting,

"AUNTY! AUNTY! Guess what! You'll never guess! I'M GOING TO BE IN THE PADGET!"

Aunty May stops treadling on her great sewing machine by the conservatory window, hurriedly whisks some blue stuff out of sight and turns round, startled at my sudden noisy entrance.

"No! Really? You've got a part? Well I never! And you won't mind being on the stage in the Hall, in front of a lot of people? And you're not bothered by that silly old twitch are you? I'm proud of you, Pieface, you're my good and clever little girl!"

"A NURSE, Aunty, I'm to be a Real Nurse cos I've got a Nurse's Outfit. Well I've lost the armbands, can I have some new ones? I have to say 'SO DO I MY DEAR' to Anthony Hodges, he's a Wounded Soldier and he's got to wear A BANDAGE! Where's Uncle Fred? I must tell him." Away down the garden screaming "UNCLE, UNCLE, GUESS WHAT! I'M TO BE A NURSE IN THE PADGET!"

It was the most wonderful Pageant EVER. Desks, blackboards, books, globes and tables were dragged down to one end, the folding screens which normally divided the classrooms lined up in front to hide it all from view, and Constitution Hall – which after all is what it says in big wooden letters above the front entrance – throws open its doors to the general public again.

Chairs placed in rows in front of the stage soon fill with families and those children that don't want to be in the Pageant, like Derek Hobbs and Ginger Beer; there's Aunty May with Uncle Fred and Santie, sitting next to Miss Crouch and oh, there's Mrs Bennett next to Reverend Dyer and Mr Benson. Mrs Benson is still round the back, along with a few fussing mums, buttoning the slower ones into their outfits, urging any who must "to 'go' now, before we start", chivvying the rest into our places on the stage; other mums are already seated and there's a sprinkling of fathers, taking an hour or so off from their farms and shops. From our side of the curtain where we are lined up ready, quivering with excitement, we can hear 'our audience' (as Miss Lucas calls them) talking softly, rustling their 'programmes' which the Big Girls have spent weeks writing out and now give to everyone coming in the door. A small group of American soldiers in uniform come in hesitantly just as we are about to start; they are quickly found seats, handed a programme, stand up politely to thank the giver and finally sit down, grinning.

The curtains rattle apart to reveal the stage swathed in patriotic red, white and blue, while Union Jacks and The Stars and Stripes hang high above us. Decked out in our costumes, each class represented by several singers, stands the Choir, littlest ones in front. Mr Wilson the Choirmaster, under whose training we have laboured, is positioned on the floor directly in front of the stage with his hands slightly raised, looking towards Mr Nichols at the piano. He nods, Mr Nichols plays the opening bars, down come Mr Wilson's arms and off we go into our first song, singing our hearts out. You can't miss me, I'm smack in the middle of the first of the two horseshoe-shaped rows round the tiny stage.

Our choir is a great success and after lots of clapping, during which Mr Wilson bows modestly twice, the individual little scenes begin. When my turn comes my tummy churns and I am shaking badly with fright and excitement. The parting curtains reveal a hospital ward with a couple of beds and blankets kindly brought down from the ARP hut in the Village and some old basket chairs from goodness knows where. The boys are 'patients', rather heavily bandaged, sitting or limping about. Wearing a dark blue dress Aunty has made specially for the occasion, with new elasticated white armbands bunching the short sleeves, and the white apron from my 'Little Nurse's Outfit' over it, I cling tightly to Anthony's arm to steady us both as he hops forward gallantly on his unbandaged leg.

"Oh Nurse" he squeaks jerkily, "I do wish this horrid War was over!"

Here it comes, My Big Chance. Stand absolutely still, face the front, look at Aunty May who, tight with suppressed pride, is nodding and mouthing encouragement.

"SO DO I MY DEAR!" I yell clear to the back of the Hall and beam round happily. My performance is greeted with smiles and murmurs, the 'aahs' and 'lit'l luvvy' audible to all. As this is the last scene before the choir comes on again for The Finale to sing God Save The King, *three* verses, for this is a Patriotic Pageant after all, the audience starts clapping before the curtains close and while the hospital beds and actors are still on the stage. Surely this time they are really applauding ME? Of course they are, I am a STAR at last.

Chapter Sixteen

"Aunty, can I ask you something?"

"Mmm? What is it? Stand up straight, dear, that's right. Now turn round, keep still. My goodness, Pieface, you *have* shot up all of a sudden! This frock's well above your knees and", pulling the yellow material round my sides, "looks a bit tight too. Well, you've had good wear out of it so I suppose this one better go for Elizabeth."

"Aunty?" Aunty May had turned back into the smaller of the two wardrobes in the spare bedroom, where me and Santie kept most of our clothes. We were occupied with the regular ritual of sorting the frocks and coats, trying them on while Aunty assessed their wearability for another six months or so. Mr Anderson had dropped a deferential word in Aunty May's ear the last time we were in his shop in Newton that there could be,

"A good quality blue gingham coming in any day now. I could – ahem – put a little piece by for the girls, enough for a little dress each perhaps? If you care to call again – next week, shall we say?"

I got very bored between each fitting while Aunty fingered first one dress, then another, holding one out, twirling it round on its little hanger. Some I wasn't even called on to try, they just went straight back in the wardrobe without comment. So, having watched the little gold balls on the clock perform their endless swing, round and back, round and back, for a while I'd been engaged in one of my favourite games, sliding down the side of the high bed on the slithery gold coverlet till Aunty said,

"Don't do that, Pieface, I've told you before, look, you're ruckling it all up. I thought you were supposed to be a big girl now." So I lolled on the window sill and fiddled with the wooden acorn on the end of the cord you pulled the blind down with.

"Oh yes, you wanted to ask me something. Ask away then, I am listening – ah, here's that flowered cotton of Santie's I was looking for, at last. I think you'll fit into it now without much taking up, come and try it on."

"Aunty, you know you sometimes say "before the War" well what does it mean? What *is* the War?"

"Of course you wouldn't remember before the War, you were still a baby then. You don't remember Grandma either, do you?" I shake my head: Grandma is known to me only as a photograph of which I am supposed to be 'the image'.

"No, Grandma went to Heaven two days before the War started, God rest her. Well for a start there wasn't any rationing then and you could go and buy anything you wanted – if you had the money of course. There was plenty of food in the shops – not that we had much, mind you; your grandad had to clean a lot of windows to feed all of us. He had to do other jobs as well because you can't keep cleaning people's windows, not more than once a week anyway, and when it rained he'd had it. Dad worked all hours to put the bread on our table. Poor old mum had her work cut out sometimes to make the pennies go round."

Aunty May sighed, staring into space. She hardly ever reminisced about the old days, in fact was more inclined to bury the past, dismissing any questions from us with a,

"That's all long ago and forgotten now."

Years later I learnt from Mum that one of Gramps' frequent jibes at Aunty – and often the cause of their many wrangles – was that because May had married well she considered herself too good for the rest of them.

Even as a child, Mum said, Aunty May had been the stuck-up one in the family, putting on airs and graces, trying to better herself. And she had done it and made them all jealous by her achievement. (Mum's own envy of Aunty was a case in point). Gramps, resentfully living in her house, was a constant reminder of humble beginnings she had magnificently risen above.

Aunty May blinked and shook herself slightly, saying,

"I'm sorry Sweetheart, I was miles away then. What were we talking about?"

"You know Barbara? Well, she told Rose that their Mum said the War might be over soon and things would be different. What things, Aunty?"

Aunty May said,

"Just turn the hem up again and it needs a couple of tucks *there* and that'll do you a treat. I'm not sure the War will be over all that soon Pieface, still who can tell? No one really knows what those politicians are doing. Put your arms up." She pulls the dress over my head and pats my ruffled cowlick of hair back into place.

"And they're certainly not going to give us any false hopes – goodness knows, we've had enough of those – not after all this long time. People are getting fed up with all their promises. Still, the News has been good for quite a while now. Our Boys seem to be doing all right, winning through at long last. What'll happen when the War's over? Well, Pieface, things will just return to normal, I suppose."

"Isn't it normal now then, Aunty? Aren't we normal?"

Aunty bends to hug me close, squashing Santie's flowered cotton which she is still holding, between us.

"Of course you're normal, you silly little thing! What I mean is, oh dear, it's so difficult to explain because you don't know anything else but blackouts and rationing and wartime. As soon as the War is over Our Boys will come home again and go back to their old jobs. We'll be able to throw our ration books away, there'll be no more rationing – or clothing coupons. And sweets will come off ration! You'll be able to get REAL chocolate again, not this fatty muck they try to pass off on us, as if we can't tell the difference indeed."

Aunty pauses, thinking, then squints down at me,

"Oranges! You'll be able to get oranges again. And B'NAH-NAS!" She draws out the word, twinkling-eyed, "You'll love bananas, Louise, you like the banana essence I put in the semolina sometimes for a change, don't you? Real bananas taste like that but a hundred times better.

"What else? Mummy and Daddy will be able to go to work properly again, without doodlebugs and bombs dropping on them. No more air-raids and sleepless nights. And you and Santie will go back to London, to new schools, and then... "

Aunty stops suddenly on an intake of breath and her face screws up, like when you've been running and get a stitch. Then she turns abruptly into the wardrobe, thrusting the frocks aside, making the hangers rattle.

"And then we'll see," she says flatly, muffled, turned away from me. "Now, why don't you go and play with your dolls' house for a while? It's really too chilly for the garden and Santie will be back soon from her Confirmation classes and we'll have tea as soon as she's in. Yes, I think we've finished in here for today. Aunty will just have a little tidy up – off you go, Sweetheart."

Perplexed by Aunty's sudden change of manner though glad to be released from trying on summer dresses in the cold room, I move towards the door and hesitate. Aunty May stands quite still, holding Santie's brown swirly skirt, watching me. She seems sad and far away, is almost looking through me and I don't know how I've upset her when she was talking so cheerfully just a moment before.

I go and squat in front of my dolls' house which lives on the landing, next to the gate-legged table, the one Santie and I get under when we want to hear Aunty and Uncle talking in the back room or secretly listen to the wireless. Of course if you want to hear *Saturday Night Theatre* on Aunty's wireless *properly* you really have to sit shivering halfway down the stairs straining your ears. *ITMA* is the easiest to listen to because Aunty has that on much louder than the plays, as she does *Music While you Work* during the day.

My dolls' house is very large with real opening windows. There is a little hook at one side and the whole front swings open on hinges so you can get at all the rooms and arrange the furniture to your satisfaction. The nicest thing about it is the 'garage' at the side with a red roof painted to look like tiles, as is the roof of the house. Lift the garage roof up and you find a round metal switch and a battery. Click! All the lights come on in every room. Magic! I don't put the lights on often though for if the battery wears out I won't be given another one. Batteries are precious: they are kept for serious things like torches for seeing your way home at night.

Street lights are unknown in our country lanes but we've got them all along The Road from Newton to Torquay, not that you'd know it because they've been turned off for ages now, the same as in London. When I asked why, Aunty said the Enemy's planes could see where we were otherwise and could bomb us. Well it worked because they haven't bombed us yet, although Newton Station was hit once and another morning Santie couldn't get to school because of all the rubbish blocking the roads after a night raid. Getting off the bus is difficult for me anyway as the step is very high and jumping down in the pitch dark rather frightening. There are no proper lights inside the bus to help you either.

In fact everything moving on the roads is blacked out, sticky strips covering half their front lights reducing them to a glimmer. Mum says even the traffic lights in London have paper crosses over them so that only a tiny bit of light shows at night, just enough to see when they change from red to green.

Perhaps I'll get a new battery when the War is over? Beautiful as my dolls' house is, it has one glaring fault: there is no staircase. I make all four members of my tiny celluloid family struggle up the side of the house to get 'upstairs'. As I like everything to be perfect, the lack of a staircase niggles.

"Why don't you just *put* all the dolls upstairs instead of walking them up the wall one at a time, you daft idiot?" asks

Santie, reasonably enough. I don't know; if I did, I wouldn't do it.

Uncle Bob, who I love almost as much as Uncle Fred, made my dolls' house. He has bright red curly hair and is Aunty Zan's husband and she is Uncle Fred's niece. Aunty Zan has the most beautiful name I ever heard but it's impossible to say – XANTHE. Nobody ever gets it right. Aunty May keeps urging, "Aunty I-ANTHEE" but Aunty Zan just laughs and says, "Aunty, so long as people don't stop speaking to me they can call me what they like!"

When Uncle Bob was home on leave the Christmas before last he came round to add the finishing touches to his handiwork. I knelt beside him, watching intently as, last lick of paint dry at last, he finally put the minute (torch) bulbs in and tested the light switch inside the garage. Aunty May said he was a brick bothering about my dolls' house when he ought to be home with Aunty Zan and Janet. As if his leave wasn't precious enough without it being Christmas too. Uncle Bob, grunting as he got up because his long legs had gone to sleep, said mildly,

"That's all right Aunty dear, I don't mind a bit. Anything for the nippers, eh? It's not their fault there's a war on, poor little things."

Aunty May said there now, wasn't I the luckiest little girl ever, to get such a lovely dolls' house? And what do you say to Uncle Bob? I said yes but it hasn't got a staircase. Aunty May's encouraging smile froze and she regarded me in angry astonishment, face pinking up. Uncle Bob bent down again and stared in, straightened up, scratching his head,

"Why, so it hasn't! Whatever were I thinking of? I'm real sorry about that Louise. Next leave I gets I'll bring my tools round and see if we can't wangle a way to fit one in. You'll have to do some redecorating afterwards though!" Uncle Bob laughed heartily, ruffling my hair while I grinned happily up at him.

Aunty May, returning down the hall after seeing him off (through the front door no less) loaded up with presents for our 'cousin-in-law' Janet, pounced on me before I had a chance to escape up the stairs.

"Well! Trust you to notice something wrong! After Uncle Bob has been so kind to make you a dolls' house in his spare time, as if he hasn't enough to do at home. How can you be so ungrateful? Whatever must he have thought? I don't understand you sometimes, Louise, always finding fault with things lately. No staircase indeed! You'll find worse things in life than missing staircases, so you might just as well get used to it, be grateful for what you've got and stop all this finickety nonsense RIGHT AWAY! As if it mattered anyway."

It mattered to me. I couldn't understand Aunty's crossness when she was such a fusspot herself. She should have been pleased after the pains she took to ensure Santie and I always replied when spoken to, told the truth and were extremely well-behaved in company. Instead I was made to feel guilty not only for pointing out the mistake to Uncle Bob but because I had *noticed* it. From that moment I knew second best would always irritate me, that I would never be happy with 'making do' and 'putting up with it'. Consequently I never really took to my dolls' house, hardly played with it at all. Needless to say, it remained staircase-less for when Uncle Bob finally came home from the War, as well as Janet and Aunty Zan, there was a new baby at his house to be taken care of and later to make wooden toys for.

"Hallo! Aunty? I'M HOME! Where is everybody?" Santie was shouting up the stairs. Auntie came out of the spare room carrying an armful of clothes, called down,

"We're coming!" and beckoned to me. I shoved everything back higgledy-piggledy into the dolls' house, swung the front shut and pushed the catch home. It had some nice furniture in its wallpapered and carpeted rooms, I must say. Daddy and

Uncle Bob had made it from matchboxes, gluing the tiny slivers into cupboards and cabinets, beds and wardrobes, little chests with real pullout drawers, all varnished shiny brown. In the 'kitchen' there was a pale orange table with a hole in the middle in which you put a teeny-weeny paper umbrella that opened and shut, and four basket chairs, all made out of celluloid.

My dolls' house family wore painted-on clothes and naturally they kept pets: a plaster dwarf, one of Snow White's seven (I sometimes wondered where the other six were) which, at 2½ inches high, was bigger than Father Doll; a china pig several times larger than the dwarf, and surprisingly, a wooden giraffe, taller even than the garage, which must have come to us from somebody else's Noah's Ark, for certainly Santie and I didn't have one.

"Oh bless the child, you've put the kettle on the trivet. Now you did use the pot-holder? I know the water's cold but the fire's VERY HOT. You were very careful?"

Santie said,

"Mais oui!" laughing as Aunty hugged her gratefully. Santie was really getting good at French though what she just said I had no idea. Aunty forbade us to go too near the open fire: even putting a shovelful of chestnuts to bake on the hob was only allowed under grown-up supervision. For Santie's arm bore several white scars, the result of grabbing at a boiling kettle when she was three years old, playing on the carpet in front of the fire. Daddy wrapped her, screaming, in a towel and ran with her to the hospital but when the towel was removed it took poor little Santie's blistered skin off with it.

"Everything all right, love?"

Santie nodded.

"What is it now? Four weeks to go? I just hope it turns warmer soon or you'll freeze to death in that white silk!

"We've been going through the wardrobe, haven't we Pieface?" Aunty told Santie, making the tea as we settled expectantly round the table. "Come on, Fred, sit down, leave that paper till later – DAD! TEA'S ON THE TABLE! Louise has grown so much lately I'm altering those" – waving her hand towards the little pile of material on the side table in front of the conservatory window – "of yours, Santie – you've mostly grown out of them anyway."

Glancing at the flowery pile, I asked,

"Can I watch you get the machine out please, Aunty? I shan't get in the way, promise."

"Well yes, if it gives you so much pleasure but you mustn't interrupt me once I've started or I'll never get finished and you won't get any supper. And we can't have that, can we?"

Aunty's side table held a secret underneath its brown velvety cover, for once this was whipped off you saw it wasn't a real table at all, just a wooden top on an iron frame with a great big wheel to one side. Aunty reached across to click something at the back and the top opened. The machine sat on a platform directly below, hidden from view by the fuzzy bobble-fringe round the edge of the cloth. Aunty pulled the machine up and the platform fitted exactly into the open space.

This was as exciting to me as Daddy's trick with the string that opened and shut the high window in the back room in London. When Aunty turned the wheel and her foot rocked the clanking treadle into life, to and fro, faster and faster, you could hear it all over the house – like a great train rushing down Dainty Bank straight to Exeter.

"We'll go through the pattern books after tea and Santie shall choose whatever style she wants – within reason of course, something sensible mind. Otherwise Louise will be well stocked up when the warmer weather comes and you won't have anything except your Special to put on and that won't last five minutes!"

Santie's Special was the white silk dress Aunty had made, with weeny pearl buttons in a row down the front. Along with Isabel and several others, Santie was to be Confirmed by the Bishop after Easter and we would all go to St. Mary's and see this wondrous happening. Santie would wear a matching white head-dress like a nurse and carry an ivory prayerbook, Aunty's

Confirmation gift. I didn't know what 'being confirmed' meant; it seemed to involve Santie going to the Church even more than usual so was obviously something else to do with God.

Judging by all the preparations and excitement shown by Aunty May, it was going to be a Big Day for Santie but for once in my life I had no wish to copy her. Since finding out that the King's Messengers had nothing to do with Our King and Queen but was a sort of weekday Sunday School I had become more wary though I envied her the white silk dress, especially the little pearl buttons.

The Bishop was known to us – indeed was a distant cousin of Uncle Fred's – sometimes calling at the house, "in passing, can't stop long, duty calls," as he put it, getting out of a large black car while his driver sat and waited, blocking the lane. The first time he visited after Santie and I were living with Aunty May, rather foolishly she didn't tell me an important visitor was expected.

The telephone rang one Saturday after tea and Aunty went into a panic, bustling and chivvying us about. Abruptly removed from my happy grubbing about in the hedge that separated Aunty's front garden from the lane, loudly protesting,

"No! What for? Don't want to. It's not fair!" I was hooked in and vigorously washed, put into a *best* frock and *clean white* socks for no apparent reason.

A Baby Jesus book thrust into my hand, I was tersely instructed to read quietly in the conservatory or on the bench in the garden, and warned,

"Don't you dare move a muscle or even *think* of getting dirty." Aunty flustered away muttering how it would be the very day Santie had gone shopping with Aunty Zan, otherwise she could have kept an eye on me.

It was a warm, hazy afternoon, buzzy and scented through the open door and suddenly quiet after the noisy washing-up of the best china and laying out of snowy-white traycloths, spitting on the hot iron to press the favoured one. Aunty had a quick whisk with the duster round the porch room and shot the blinds up in the drawing room. It was obvious even to one as self-absorbed as me that Someone Important was coming.

Baby Jesus soon palled and the garden beckoned enticingly. Sit on a bench, Aunty said. Which one? On the front lawn of course, the first to welcome Miss Crouch or perhaps those two nice American Soldiers with all the medals were coming to visit us again? The birds twittered, time passed. Daydreaming, I forgot why I was sitting there and eventually wandered off to look at the snail shells a thrush had left on one of the boulders that bordered the driveway.

"Just like getting a winkle out with a pin," Mum had said, watching as the thrush held a snail in its beak, banging it down on the rock repeatedly till its shell shattered and he pecked out the contents.

Gathering up small flat pebbles, I squatted down on the step which led off the driveway on to the narrow path in front of the house, and began to play Five Stones. I was very good at Five Stones: like embroidery, it needed a lot of concentration to keep your arm steady enough to catch the pebbles on the back of your hand when you threw them up.

Absorbed in the game, I didn't hear the big car come purring up the lane nor the gate click. There was a soft swishing behind me and someone said,

"Hello, my child. Five Stones eh? I used to play that when I was about your age. Let's see if I can still do it."

On a level with my eyes was a pair of shining black gaiters and, looking up, a large silver cross swung close to my head. An old man with a lined, soft face was smiling down, stooping creakily to crouch by my side. Always peeved at being interrupted, if it was Santie or Edward I shouted angrily, giving them a shove. But this was a grown-up and I wouldn't dare give a grown-up the sharp end of my elbow. So I silently pushed the stones towards him.

He threw them up, spreading out a wrinkly hand which had a large red ring on it. He wore a purple shirt under his black jacket which Aunty May would never wear because, she said,

"Purple was such a difficult colour, like navy – never two shades the same."

He dropped four of the stones, tried again, got three on this time. Wiggling his fingers to drop two off he dropped all three. Had another go. Got one. Gave up.

"No," he said, struggling to his feet, "I'm too out of practice. You better show me how to do it."

He stood on the driveway, stooped, watching closely. Throw up five stones, catch on back of hand, wiggle fingers, drop all but one. Toss it up, catch in palm. Toss, pick up singles, one-no-miss. Toss, pick up in twos, put quickly down, catch pebble. Toss, three-and-one, down, catch, then toss and grab all four together. Keeping the pebbles close together when you put them down was the trick or you scrabbled about blindly, eyes following the tossed-up stone thrown too high so you couldn't catch it and were Out.

The man was very admiring.

"You're far better at this than I am, my little friend, and SO DEXTROUS! Oh dear, there's Mrs Sherwood looking for me, I'm afraid I've kept her waiting. I must leave you to your game but I'll try again next time I'm here. My *dear* May, how good to see you again. Is this one of your nieces? What a dear little thing, so sad, St Vitus has a lot to answer for. 'Suffer the little children' indeed. Still, having young ones about us is such a comfort in these troubled times, I always think." And in he swept, ushering Aunty red-faced before him.

Aunty May, on the lookout, had seen the Bishop come half-way up the drive and then seemingly disappear off the face of the earth. Stepping through the front door to sort out this mystery, she was appalled to find that I was not sitting piously reading as instructed but instead was squatting on the path playing FIVE STONES IF YOU PLEASE! And, horror of horrors, there was Cousin Bishop quite unable to get past and having to ask me to move out of his way!

Aunty May fairly went for me when he'd gone – well, I'd Shown Her Up, hadn't I?

"Stuck in his way like that, sitting on the path of all things, I could hardly believe my eyes. No wonder he asked you to get up."

"He NEVER, Aunty! He never said *anything* like that. He asked me to show him how to play, so I did. It's true!"

Aunty snapped,

"Don't tell lies, as if he would!"

"It's *true*, I'm *not* lying! He said I was *much* better than him! He said I'm DESK-TOSS! Honest, Aunty, HE DID!"

I was shouting, desperate to make her understand but Aunty didn't want to know, preferred her version of the scene to the truth. She wasn't being fair, wouldn't listen, was so cross you'd think the old man must be as important as the King, the fuss she made. Unjustly accused, I cried bitterly till Aunty calmed down, kissed and comforted me and another storm passed.

The next time Cousin Bishop rang to say he would call in passing and couldn't stop I was warned in advance and kept well out of the way, sitting in the conservatory so good and still that Aunty May couldn't have wished for a better-behaved girl. No, not even Little Shirley Temple herself.

Chapter Seventeen

"Santie, do you want to go to a new school?"

"What new school? What are you talking about?"

Standing in the sun on the front path in our best costumes, although it was far too hot for navy wool, I watched Aunty May fiddling with her Brownie Box, peering down into it then up at us several times.

"Move in a bit, Louise", she flapped her hand at me like the policeman in Torquay did at the bottom of Union Street. I moved in a bit. Aunty looked into her camera again, cupped her hand round the top and called,

"Try and stand still, there's a good girl, I'll only be a minute. Hold her hand Santie, that's it. Now that's lovely – SMILE! This one's for Mummy. Louise, you're squinting again. Oh well, too late, I've taken it now," winding the film on, "better take another one, just to make sure."

"I don't know why Aunty bothers, you know what Daddy says about her snaps," Santie murmurs, letting go my hand. "Besides, she's taken us standing here like this hundreds of times. I'm sweltering. AUNTY," she calls, "can we put something else on? It's boiling in these costumes."

"That's because you're standing in the sun. There's still a nasty wind about. It's not summer yet, you know. You can put a blouse on for now though because I want those jumpers kept clean for later – and put an apron over that skirt Louise, you know what a Muckworm you are. Can't leave you alone for five minutes before you're into something."

That's true. I don't know how it happens but whenever I'm in the garden – even just standing still – dirt sort of jumps up and sticks to me. Buffed up ready to go out, checked over from head to toe before leaving the house, having done nothing but walk holding Aunty or Mum's hand to the station or bus-stop, my face is suddenly tipped up and examined closely. Angrily demanding,

"Whatever have you been doing? Look at you!" and despite my protests, they spit on a hanky, scrubbing it hurtfully round my mouth till my chin goes red. Now I am cross and grumpy, the pleasure in the outing spoiled and I get told off for scowling.

Chewing a piece of chives, watching Santie picking bluebells to put in the jam jar on our table in the White House, I ask,

"What does Daddy say about Aunty's snaps then?"

"'Lovely view of the road, May' usually," Santie laughs. Once he said, 'it's a pity you just got the girls in the corner of this one, spoilt the beauty of that old hedge and empty field'. You know how fussy Daddy is about taking photographs, makes you wait ages while he gets it just right. He told Mum that Aunty hadn't a straight eye and shouldn't be allowed within ten miles of a camera. Stop eating the chives," snatching it out of my hand, "your breath'll smell horrible. Oh look, here's a pink bluebell. A 'Pinkbell' I suppose; let's show it to Aunty."

After dinner, lying on my bed listening to a bee suzzling behind the pulled-down blind, Santie tiptoed quietly into the room. Turning my head to smile at her she grinned back and, pushing the door to, plumped down next to me saying,

"Good, you're awake – tell me, who said anything about new schools?"

"Aunty did, the other day. Will you let that bee out the window for me?"

"Sure." Upping the window she crooned, "off you go little bee, out into the sunshine – shall I leave it open a crack? It's so hot in here. I don't know what Aunty means, you must have got it all wrong as usual. She's said nothing to me though of course you'll have to leave St Mary's after the Scholarship, like I did. I shall stay at The High till I'm sixteen then I'll go to drama school, Daddy says I can, and I'll be a famous actress and earn pots of money."

"Aunty did say it, Sant, honest. 'After the War you'll both go to new schools' that's what she said. When I asked why, she didn't answer, just sent me off to play."

"Oh I get it, she means when we go back to London. I'll still go to the same school though, the one they evacuated and dumped on us at Newton."

I stared at her, unbelieving. This was amazing news indeed. I knew there were Vaccees at Santie's school, same as Lily, and Pat Morris in dear Miss Digby's, oh and the Revell Twins, Eric and Arthur in Edward's class but Santie said they moved a SCHOOL. First time I'd heard of it. I sat up.

"A whole school? All the teachers and the classrooms as well? Cor! You never told me it was two schools, you never said."

"Oh honestly Lou, everybody knows that. Sometimes I *despair* of you." She sounded just like Aunty May. "It's not just the local kids who go to my school, there's tons of others as well." She spoke lightly, off-hand. "Loads of schools were evacuated and Newton got one from South London, quite near to where Mum and Dad live luckily. I shall carry on at the High School but in London instead of Newton, that's all. Anyway, we are FAR superior, us *London* girls, than the others – they're so SLOW. We have competitions in class and in Games or Swimming and that, WE win every time."

Most of Sant's airy school talk went right over my head. Struggle though I might to keep up with her my mind was completely taken up with a whole big building being moved from one place to another. It must have taken ages to get on the train at Paddington with all the girls and desks and the teachers carrying the blackboards. I'd have to have a good think about that later, sort it out in my own way. I don't know what she means about going to the High School in London either. Will I go there too?

"I don't want to go to school in London and anyway I'm going with you to Newton after the Scholarship, Aunty said. I can't see why we have to go all the way to London. It takes ever so long to get there and it's dark and smells nasty and there's no fields, nowhere to play."

"No, silly, we'll be living with Mum and Dad then, we won't live here anymore. I don't want to go back either, not really, but we'll have to do as we're told as usual, we don't have any say in the matter. You wait, when I'm grown up I shall do exactly as I want instead of what other people tell me to and no one shall stop me, no never."

Santie narrows her eyes, contemplating her future of complete freedom. Then she says casually,

"By the way, Lou, don't tell anybody what I said about the London girls at school, being superior I mean. I have to pretend I'm one of them 'cos they know my best friends come from the Village and if I side with the local lot they make fun of us."

"What do they do?" Curiosity compels me to interrupt but she doesn't seem to notice, just glances at me with troubled eyes,

"Mm-m? Oh, point at us in the street, call out 'there go the Village Idiots' or 'look at the Hayseeds', that sort of thing. Josie's all right, she's in the same boat as me, lives with her Mum and Aunty over Milber. Got bombed out a couple of years ago and came down here. Though they're not from London, Bristol or somewhere like that – anyway it began with a 'B'. But London doesn't mean anything to me now, it's so long ago since we lived there. I just say it's better than the country to keep in with the girls at school. It's a lie really, I don't want to live anywhere else but here, ever. Promise you won't tell? About pretending?"

I'm only half-listening now, still fretting over going to London to a school I don't know, but I see Santie's bright blue eyes turned on me anxiously and realise she's asked me to pretend to tell somebody at school – what? Or did she say not to tell? Oh crumbs, I don't know whether to nod Yes or shake No. I shake my head tentatively and she beams with obvious relief.

I wonder vaguely who she doesn't want me to tell: apart from Isabel who always smiles hallo at me, there's only Mary Tancock, Sheila and Verity from Santie's school who live round here – oh and Josie Withers at Swimming, and I wouldn't dare speak to any of them without permission.

Josie and swimming send my mind sliding down a side lane and I say, for no apparent reason,

"Will you take me to the Penguin Paddling Pool again soon?"

Santie has got up, stands smoothing down her skirt which she's really grown out of, it's well above her knees now – looks like I'll get that one handed down and be wearing navy costumes for ever. She stares at me.

"Whatever made you say that? What's the paddling pool got to do with anything, you daft 'aporth? Have you been listening to a word I've said?"

We are silent for a while. Santie has lost interest for she turns now to peer in the mirror, wetting her fingers to push back the hated baby curl dangling on her forehead. Some of her words start repeating in my head and there's a prickle of fear in my tummy as I slowly ask,

"D'you mean we won't come home again next time we go up to London, to Mum and Dad? We'll have to stay there for good? For ever and ever? Oh no, Santie, that CAN'T be true, say it isn't."

"I dunno, it all depends – when the War's over, what happens I mean. Perhaps Aunty May'll keep us here, at least till I'm sixteen and go to drama school; well I'll have to go to London for that of course."

She sighs, flicking at a dandelion clock floating towards the chest of drawers, making it dance upwards over my head, silvery and shining.

"Whatever happens you can bet your life there'll be a row because I know for a fact Aunty May won't let us go without a fight. She and Mum'll go at it hammer and tongs and I expect Mum'll win, she usually does. All the same I miss Daddy

172

dreadfully, don't you? D'you want to come down now? I'm sure Aunty won't mind if we go and sit in the White House till we're called to get ready, I'll ask her."

"Get ready for what? Not Church again, please – we've already been once this morning and it's too late for Sunday School. What's happening?"

"Aunty Zan's coming to tea, it's her birthday today – soon, I dunno; anyway Aunty May has made a cake." Santie calls over her shoulder, starting down the stairs. "We'll have to play with Janet after I suppose, so they can chinwag, now she's carrying. I wanted to go round Isabel's – some hopes! Oh how I hate Sundays."

"What's she carrying?" I ask, following her on to the landing for I'm busting to 'go' and must use Upstairs or make a puddle.

"Her shopping," Santie laughs and pausing at the top of the stairs, says,

"Louise, what you said just now about the Penguin Pool, I've just had a thought. Tell you what, if you promise to play with Janet this afternoon by yourself, leave me out of it, then perhaps – I won't promise mind – perhaps, if Aunty says it's all right, I might take you next time I go."

Actually Santie hated having to take me to the Babies' pool especially if her school pals were at the Baths. It cut down her swimming time with them having to keep a watchful eye on me splashing happily a few yards away, like a fat wet wasp in my knitted costume of black and yellow stripes.

Delighted, I run and hug her before dashing urgently into the lavatory, giving the door a great joyful slam. Aunty calls from below,

"Oh you're up, are you? Stop slamming that door, making such a row, behave yourself and WASH YOUR HANDS!"

While we're playing Snap in the White House, a sudden honking brings us out the door as two white geese fly overhead.

I shudder, the thought of their nasty beaks inches behind my fleeing legs forever in my memory. Santie says,
"Look out, you might get a bit of luck in your eye! Good job cows don't fly!"
Her bubbly snort screams out into great guffaws then, as we resume our seats she says, quite casually,
"Did I ever tell you how I got chased by a cow?"
"No you never! A COW? Cows don't chase you, it must've been a bull. Where? When? Tell me!"
"It was definitely a cow and it'd just had a calf. It was before your time, when I went to the Village School. I was going past the gate next to Honeypots – where we cow-stepped, remember? Well I cow-stepped, you fell in – and Old Stanton's cart was there to fetch the calf in. Born during the night I suppose."
She leans forward, fixing her eyes on a distant spot in her past while I wait, twitching, scared to speak in case she decides not to continue.
"Anyway, just as I got there Kenneth Stanton came out of the field carrying a lovely little calf, puts it in the cart and leaves the gate open.
"'Shall I shut the gate for you?' I shouted and he said, 'No, stay back' but before I has a chance to, the cow sees me and reckons it's me that's pinching her calf.
"She comes bellowing out the gate, straight past the cart before Kenneth can stop her and I tore down the lane with her after me. You'd never believe how fast a cow can go! I ran all the way to school without stopping and when I got through the gate I was puffed out. There was a crowd of kids in the yard and I screamed,
'There's a cow chasing after me!' and d'you know what they rotten well did? They LAUGHED at me, started jeering 'Townee! Scared of a cow-ow! Scared of a cow-ow!' I never told anyone, not even Aunty, but I hated all of them for a long time. I wouldn't be scared now, of course, I was only little then."

"Oh Santie," I gasp, "how awful! You're s-o-o brave, I couldn't have done that, run all the way to school. I'd have just DIED, I know I should."

"Oh I don't know, you got chased by the geese, I felt quite sorry for you at the time, reminded me of that old cow." She smiles kindly at me, soaking up my adoration, assured of the gloss the five-year age gap gives her.

I want her to go on with more stories but she's picked up the cards again, saying,

"Is it my turn?" so in desperation I ask,

"What happened to the cow?"

"Ay?" She comes down from her cloud with a bump. "I don't know, oh yes, Kenneth Stanton caught up with it on the bridge and tied her to the back of the cart so she could see the calf and Dora (Old Stanton's fat black mare) took them back to the farm."

"Did the Italeyans see it? On the railway? By the side of the bridge? Did they call out 'beller-beller' at you?"

"This was *age-es* ago I'm talking about, they weren't even here then. And anyway I wasn't going to stop and say,

"'Good morning how are you?' with a cow chasing me, was I, you ninny? Listen, isn't that Aunty calling?" She glances through the open door and yells, "OK, we're coming!" at the top of her voice, making me jump out of my skin, for I am still mentally tearing over the bridge with a cow breathing fire behind me.

The Italians working on the railway were there most days when I came home from school but I never stopped for, to tell the truth, I was a little afraid of them. But Santie always paused to hang over the bridge, shouting hallo, whereupon the men started grinning and waving to her, gabbling in a strange language I'd never heard before.

Too small to see over the parapet and not allowed to climb up its stone sides though there were plenty of toeholds, I would peep nervously through the wire gaps in the broken wooden palings at the side, watching them. One day they spotted me

peering through the cow parsley and started laughing and one
called,
"Ah-h-h, leetel leetel wun," patting his chest, where your
heart is. Then they all jabbered, "beller-beller, beller-beller"
pointing at Santie then me.
"Come on Santie, come away. I don't like them, I want to
go." Whining again, pulling at the back of Santie's coat,
anxious to dislodge her.
"Don't do that you fool, you'll have me over," she shrugged
me off crossly, jumping down backwards on to the road.
"What are you afraid of anyway? They can't hurt you, they're
prisoners aren't they. I feel sorry for them having to work here
with nobody to talk to. How d'ya think they feel? Anyway, *I*
like them, they're nice and friendly; and it's no good moaning
like that, Scaredy-cat, I shall stop and say hallo every single
time. So there!"

Now, head whirling with the cow and the Italians I follow
Santie in and allow myself to be tidied up for the expected
visitors without protest. Indeed I am so thoughtful that Aunty
asks if I have another headache, oh dear she hopes not; am I
sure? She narrows her eyes, unconvinced, says I'm too quiet
for her liking. She always says this when she thinks I might be
'up to something'.
Unmindful of my promise after the jolly tea party (no sign
of the cake Aunty's supposed to have made though), I'm
enjoying myself, listening to the chatter, straining to find out
more details as they talk of the War and when it might all be
over, when bidden by Aunty May to take Janet to the garden
for a while as the sun's out, to get a bit of air. I'm whining,
"It's not fair, do we have to?" when I catch sight of Santie's
unblinking blue eyes fixed on me. Quickly scrambling up I
hurry Janet round to the front lawn and we make daisy-chain
necklaces for our dolls, sitting on the old green bench, legs
swinging in unison.

I don't mind her really; a year or so younger than me with long blonde curls which I greatly envy, my own head at that time exhibiting only "two hairs and a nit" according to Mum who has just received photographic evidence of the too-short haircut Aunty May recently gave me. Janet was bright, inquisitive and giggly. We got on quite well together considering she was still a bit babyish and wouldn't join in anything that might make her frock or shoes dirty. Needless to say Aunty May approved of her highly.

Still it was a relief when Santie tapped on the drawing room window and beckoned us in. We ran into the kitchen just as Aunty May picked up a big tray and there after all was The Cake, some glasses and her bottle of 'O T' ginger wine.

"Mind out! What have I said about running? Wash your hands, you two – Louise, get the stool, help Janet up to the sink, that's it, remember when you couldn't reach the tap either? Then follow me, we're in the drawing room."

"Can I have some 'O T' as well Aunty, please?" Ever hopeful, eyeing the bottle. She always said "you won't like it" or "it's not for children". But not this time.

"Perhaps just a thimbleful then, to celebrate," Aunty twinkled at me and Janet, quite unlike her rather formal demeanour when anyone was there. "So hurry yourselves up before it all goes."

Carefully sipping my teeny-weeny glassful, for it was very strong, with a mouth full of cake and staring at the bottle on the silver tray I asked,

"Why does it say 'O T'?"

And Aunty said,

"Because it's 'OT'!" and we laughed and laughed. I saved it up to tell Daddy next time he came down.

Everybody so happy – even Gramps, jiggling Janet up and down on his knee – and the ginger wine, reserved for very special occasions, making an appearance meant today was more than just Aunty Zan's birthday. As usual no one thought to tell me why, their mistaken belief being that too young to understand I also saw and heard nothing. Indeed their very secrecy alerted my curiosity: sharp ears picking up whispered words here and there, ever-watchful eyes noticing significant glances between the Aunties. Even Santie seemed in on it. Nor had I failed to spot the bump in front of Aunty Zan as soon as she came into the house. I knew what THAT meant, just about. I would be eight next birthday, listening and learning from playground gossip, and whatever Santie said that bump certainly wasn't Aunty Zan's shopping. Still I could pretend with the best of them and when Santie nudged me to stop staring, it's rude, Aunty Zan has just eaten too much, I didn't even bother to argue.

During the next few days going to a strange school in London worried at me like a dangly tooth and I wondered whether Santie had spoken to Aunty. But time passed, nothing more was said and gradually my fears faded into the gentle, familiar patterns of School, Church and Village, dawdling along the lanes, playing in the fields, shopping in Newton and going 'treats' to the Pictures with Santie on Saturday afternoons.

The sun grows hotter, summer's almost here and one breezy morning, smiling at the pegged sheets flinging themselves over the washing line, billowing pillowcases as fat as barrage balloons, Aunty says,

"What a wonderful day! It's just the sort of morning when you fancy a kipper for your tea." I don't understand so just nod happily up at her beaming face, handing up the next peg at the exact moment her hand swings down to take it. I'm extremely good at this, no one can do it better, Aunty says. Suddenly she grabs both my hands and, holding them tight, swings me joyfully round like the washing dancing above my head, over the narrow path in an aeroplane ride.

Chapter Eighteen

Santie is shaking me awake. Far away I hear Aunty May saying,

"That's it, wake her up Santie. Louise! Come on, love, get up quickly."

There is a strange glow lighting up the room but it can't be getting-up time as Aunty is still in her dressing-gown.

"Ish it an air-raid?" Fuzzy with sleep, lisping through my missing front tooth (the Fairy came yesterday and took it away, leaving a shiny threepenny bit under my pillow) I struggle up.

"No, but I want you both outside. Put your knickers and vest on, now arms up," as a jumper is pulled over my sleepy head, "and slip this skirt on. You too Santie, get dressed quickly, that's right, good girl, while I run and put my top things on."

A few minutes more and Aunty bundles us out, pushing us ahead of her, calling "DAD! ARE YOU DOWN YET?" as we stumble down the stairs. "Good, there's your Uncle, waiting with the coats."

Downstairs? This doesn't look good – are we to sit under the stairs, in that gloomy airless cupboard with the mice and creepy things which I hate more than the air-raids? But wait, this is very odd: although it's still dark the back door stands wide open. A shadowy figure, must be Gramps, clomps ahead of us as Aunty ushers us out.

"Go round into the lane both of you, Uncle and I are right behind. Fred, have you got Ginger's basket? Bring her along too though she'll probably run off under the shed but at least she's out of the house."

The red glow is more evident outside the house and there is a loud crackling noise. My nostrils twitch at the acrid, smoky smell of – something large, burning.

"Hey, look!" Santie, ahead of me, cries out as she rounds the corner on to the drive, "Miller's hayrick's on fire!"

Gosh, this is exciting. Running down to the gate I can hear the fire engine clanging along the lower road from Newton. There seem to be loads of people from the Village with our neighbours in the lane as well as Mr Miller and Tom. Seeing Edward, a couple of boys from school and the two landgirls from Stanton's farm standing on top of the hedge across the lane, Santie and I clamber up to join them for a better view. Aside from calling out,

"Be careful, you two and stay well back, keep with Edward," Aunty May, on the path by the front door, doesn't stop us – in fact rather elaborately waves us on.

Gramps has gone to get the seldom-used hosepipe, running it off the tap in the kitchen but it doesn't reach anywhere near the blazing hayrick. The bit of garden under the hedge that separates us from Miller's field gets an unexpected and unauthorised watering before Uncle Fred plods back round to tell Gramps not to bother. By the time the fire engine grinds up the lane there is no rick left but the hedge by our gate has caught fire so they turn their official hose on that, dousing it quickly.

Faces lit up momentarily by the glare merge once again into the surrounding darkness as the fire dies down and our neighbours begin to drift back home in little groups, talking quietly together until we can't hear them anymore and only a thin column of smoke is left, with me and Santie and the puddles in the lane. Mr Miller, who has spent the entire time doing nothing but wailing about 'me mangoils' and waat's he to do now, stands irresolutely until Mrs A kindly brings him and Tom a cup of tea. There being nothing else to watch except a bit of smouldering stubble, Aunty comes to get us in and we reluctantly climb down.

"Good job it's a warm night or we'd have all caught our deaths standing out here at two o'clock in the morning," Aunty chatters us in. Uncle Fred, making one of his rare comments, laughs suddenly and says,

"Reckon it were *too* warm a night for Old Miller if you asks me anything!"

Tucking us back into bed, I ask,

"What's mangoils?"

"Mangel-wurzels – you know, old turnips, for Mr Miller's cows to eat in the winter. He stored them in the middle of the rick; I reckon that's how it started, they get too hot, start burning and up goes the lot. That or could've been a cigarette-end not put out properly – he smokes like a chimney anyway. Now straight off to sleep, it's very late and you've still got school in the morning. Still, won't you have something to write to Mummy and Daddy about in your letters this week?"

Mummy had something to say too when she wrote back to Aunty May for this time I actually saw the letter. Aunty left it lying on the table when Mrs A tapped at the back door and she went to see what she wanted. Not slow to grasp an opportunity, the bit I managed to read before she came back said,

" ...her spelling isn't any better, what's a hitge when it's at home? Why get them up in the middle of the night to watch a fire, S says they stood on a hedge in the lane, where's the sense in that? I know it was next door to you May but nowhere near the house. I've a good mind to... "

That's all I had time to see before the back door shut and Aunty returned to find me innocently looking out the drive-side window down to our blackened bit of hedge at the bottom.

"Ready for school then?" she said brightly, "if you're really too tired you can stay home this morning if you want."

"I'm all right Aunty, really. Anyway Edward's coming; this is his last term, he's going to the Grammar School." Tired or not, of course I'd go, couldn't wait to get there with my exciting night's news. I certainly didn't want to miss the chance of lording it over them at playtime.

Now it's June again, Aunty May's birthday, time for another carefully coloured card from me (a dark brown caravan this year with yellow wheels which Mrs Moffatt cut out in such a way that it stood up – "very realistic" Aunty said). It is popped up on the mantelpiece among the photographs of Aunty Zan and Janet, Uncle Bob in his uniform, Uncle Fred in Lay Reader's cassock and frilled collar. There was 'a studio portrait' of Santie and me done in Torquay, and a brown picture from a long time ago, a hay wagon with lots of men with moustaches sprawled on it, staring out at me whenever I looked up.

"That's Uncle Fred in the middle, when he was a young man, long before I knew him," Aunty said, lifting it down for me to see better. "It was their annual outing from the Railway, he did tell me where they went that day but I don't remember. Anyway, that's him, doesn't he look handsome?"

Well if you looked close you could see it was somebody a bit like Uncle Fred but with a black moustache and dark hair showing under the wide-brimmed hat tipped to the back of his head. I liked him best in the cassock, silver hair shining, just as he was now.

The sun shone hotly day after day and grown-ups grumbled at the lack of rain when the farmers and vegetables were "crying out for it" according to everyone except me and Santie, who love summer best of all; the way the lane shone in the heat, the big bubbles that suddenly came up in the tar and oozed blackly over my sandals as I squashed as many as I could.

Santie took me to the Penguin Baths several times and then it started to rain heavily just as Mum and Dad came down to spend a week with us in July.

"You brought it with you Grace," Aunty May told Mum cheerfully as they walked up the wet drive, Daddy behind with an arm round each of us and the man from the garage following with their cases. "Not that we couldn't do with it, been dry as dust down here for days on end."

"Better that than those blessed doodlebugs Jerry's sending us now, as if we didn't have enough on our plates already. I tell you May... " but they'd gone through the top gates and round the house so I didn't hear anymore.

"What's a Blessed Doodlebug?" I ask Daddy. It must be something to eat if it's on a plate and Mum's said 'For What We Are About To Receive' before starting.

"A flying bomb. A tiny aeroplane flies over quite low with a fiery tail like a comet and as it goes over it makes a loud buzzing noise. When the noise stops you wait for the doodlebug to fall and pray for it not to fall on you this time."

'Doodlebug' is such a nice word that I start to laugh but Daddy looks so serious and sad that I let go his arm and run on ahead, to clamour round Mummy instead.

By August the farmers were keeping anxious eyes on the sky, judging the right moment to start cutting their corn, warily watching for mares' tails in the vast blue saucer for the higher the thin cloud trails remained, the better. Everybody turned out to help LEND A HAND ON THE LAND, as the posters urged, to get the harvest safely home. In the field opposite Aunty's house, next to Bobs and Charley's grassy meadow, Santie worked hard too, one of many 'stookers', gathering up the cut corn into sheaves and stacking them two by two, tops touching, so they leant against one other like rows and rows of little pointed arches.

I was too little to help and anyway it was more fun running in and out of the stooks with the other children, screaming and chasing each other with tickly bits of straw. Covered in dust, scratched and stained, happy till Aunty puts me in the bath and gets the flannel round the cuts on my legs and arms. Then the tears start and out comes the Dettol and sticking plasters.

When the last square of standing corn remained in the middle of the field, Santie grabs me saying,

"Come on, Lou, indoors!" hustling me into the house. Other children were made to keep with their mums, well out of the way. This is the part of the day Santie dreaded. She's never told me why so this year I break free from her and run upstairs to hang out of our window. I see the corn falling behind the cutter and as the square gets smaller and smaller out run dozens of rabbits. "Get away from the window, Lou," Santie screams from the stairs, "don't look!" Too late. BANG! BANG! Oh, no, the men are shooting the dear little bunnies, laughing, picking them up as they fall. It's horrible, I wish I hadn't looked and run sobbing out on the landing.

Santie's arms are round me, her tears falling as fast as mine.

"I told you not to watch, Lou but you wouldn't listen – don't cry now, it's all over and the rabbits didn't suffer, not like when they're caught in traps and scream all night. There, dry your eyes on my hanky, I've still got to finish stooking – mustn't let the other kids see we've been crying they'll only laugh at us."

The Harvest Festival at St Mary's was lovely, even better than Christmas; loaves and vegetables and a big tin of Spam, and Uncle Fred's huge striped marrows lying with shiny red tomatoes and luscious apples in heaps along the steps in front of the screen. But when we stood singing happily 'All Is Safely Gathered In' and I looked at the two big sheaves of corn leaning either side of the pulpit I remembered the rabbits running for dear life and the noise of the guns. And oh dear, this is dreadful: instead of helping to 'Raise the Song of Harvest Home' my head's singing, 'Run Rabbit, Run Rabbit, Run Run Run; Don't Get the Farmer his Gun, Gun, Gun.' I'm twitching madly, grimacing, trying not to burst out laughing.

Just before Harvest Festival my long-awaited birthday arrives at last. I am eight now, soon be grown-up like Santie and I feel different, older, braver. I might even say hallo to the Italians, well perhaps, one day. Older I may be yet despite what Aunty says I don't seem any taller than last year when I was seven and had a real birthday party. I'd looked forward to that party for so long and yet when Margaret and Christine, Audrey and Rose of course, Edward from next door, Aunty Zan and Janet and Isabel to keep Santie company arrived there were too many people in the crowded drawing room and I got over-excited, tearful and silly and my head ached. Once I'd opened my presents I wished they'd all go away and leave me to play on my own.

I'm not having a party this year but I don't mind, I'm still the centre of attention. It is a soft, gentle September day and Aunty May takes us all to Honeypots for a special tea where they've made me a dear little cake as a surprise, with eight candles on it.

"Better than a bit of bread and cheese and a slide round the plate, as Mum would say," Santie whispers, digging me in the ribs with her surprisingly sharp elbow, just as I am about to lean over and blow out my candles so that I collapse giggling and have to start again.

Swinging among the apple trees out over the hidden railway lines, dreaming, I finger the lacy frills round the sleeves of my new birthday frock and stare up at the blue endless sky, happy and contented for there are no bulls to worry about at Honeypots and the geese are safely locked away, thank goodness. Down the lane blackberries ripen in the late summer sun, fat and shiny black; time to get the baskets out. I've seen one or two pickers already near the school but unless I'm picking with Rose to fill our own mouths and leave smudgy stains on fingers and frocks, Santie and I never pick further than our end of the lane, to the corner one way and Mrs A's the other.

"Leave some on for others," Aunty always says, "don't take them all." But hardly anyone comes this far out from the Village so really we have the whole lane to ourselves.

Hazel nuts, which I love even more than apples, are ready too. The best ones grow in the hedge the other side of Mrs A's, branches bowed low so I can reach quite easily. But only Santie and me, Uncle Fred and Edward know this favoured spot and we pick together, in amicable secrecy.

To get the best chestnuts you have to go further, up the side lane that leads on to The Road. Two immense trees stand on a

small triangle of open grass bordering it near the bus-stop to
Newton. There's no gate here, just a large broken gap in the
hedge and we join several others picking up the prickly casings.
You need thick gloves for this job but you still get spikes in
your fingers, right through the layers of wool. It's worth it
though when you get back and Aunty slits the nuts and puts
them on an old shovel on the trivet to roast.

One cold evening Santie pleaded to be allowed to do the
chestnuts by ourselves and reluctantly, with strict instructions
to,

"Take care with the fire, remember your poor old arm,"
Aunty agreed; we got the shovel and tipped the nuts on. Then
we forgot about them. After a little while there was an
immense bang and Gramps jumped up, cussing at us. His
slipper, habitually dangling off his heel as he sat reading the
paper next to the fire, had received a hot chestnut and even
now a smell of singeing filled the air. Of course in jumping up
he put his heel right down on the blackened chestnut which
made him so angry that he kicked the slipper clean across the
room.

"You bloody kids!" he yelled at us, "you did that on
purpose, I know you!" Aunty May, hearing the commotion
from above, came flying into the room, snatching the shovel off
the fire, for chestnuts were exploding on to the carpet at a
terrific rate. Scared out of our wits, Santie and I fled to the
kitchen while Aunty placated Gramps,

"Now, now Dad, she didn't mean it and you're not hurt.
There's no real harm done."

"What about me slipper then? Bloody great hole in it!
Who's paying for a new pair? Not her, oh no, I'll be bound.
You oughter stop it out of her pocket money till I gets a new
pair, little madam."

"Honestly, Dad, you're worse than a baby the fuss you
make. Santie's forgotten to slit the skins, I should have done
them or at least given eye to her before I went upstairs. It's
your own fault anyway, you will sit too near with your slipper

hanging off like an old tramp but you won't take a blind bit of notice."

Any further words from Gramps were drowned by the clatter of Aunty's hearth brush sweeping up the bits and when Gramps stumped upstairs muttering,

"Always sides with them, never mind about me," we crept back. The only noticeable damage was a couple of small scorch marks on the thick carpet. Aunty, getting up off her plump round knees, said,

"Well! That's the last time you do chestnuts – I know you didn't mean it but you'll still have to say sorry to your Grandad when he's calmed down; I'll buy him another pair of slippers. It would have to be you upsetting him, wouldn't it?" Aunty sighed, hugging Santie close, stroking her curls. "He'll come round, love, never fear. It's a funny thing though; the day after you were born Gramps went out and bought Rupert for you, the biggest teddy-bear he could find he said. Did you know that? He never did that for any of the grandchildren before – or since, come to that. So you see Santie, he does care for you really, in his own way."

Surprised though she was by the news that Rupert (who stood nearly two feet high and growled softly when you bent him over) had been Gramps' present not Daddy's as she had always understood, Santie remained unconvinced of Gramps' apparent caring attitude towards her. So did I.

Before October starts to slide into winter, while the days are still warm though there's a definite nip in the air when we get up each morning, Aunty says one Saturday night, as I'm going up to bed,

"By the way Pieface, Uncle Fred's going mushrooming tomorrow morning, early mind, and I expect Santie'll go with him. Do you want to go too?"

"OF COURSE I DO!"

"All right, all right, there's no need to yell like that. Only you seem to spot them in the grass much quicker even than Santie does, Uncle says."

"That's because she's much nearer the ground than anybody else." Santie says, coming in from the kitchen. "She hardly has to bend down, old Titchy-titch."

"Now Santie, don't be unkind, Louise can't help being short. You wait, one day she'll start shooting up and probably be taller than any of us, I wouldn't mind betting." I didn't and am not.

I love picking mushrooms, searching in the cold morning air for the shining white buttons in the grass at the bottom of Bobs and Charley's field where it damply slopes to the wooden fence and steep banking of the railway line. Their strange earthy smell, the indescribably soft feel of their little brown gills as you slide your fingers down the stalk to gently twist them from their hiding place.

After watching Aunty tip our full baskets on to the kitchen table, wiping each mushroom carefully with a damp cloth before slicing and popping them in the pan to sizzle, I lose interest. I tried a bit once, didn't like it. Still don't.

The approach of Christmas is heralded by Aunty May getting out last year's paper chains to see if they'll do another turn or need repairing; whereupon she sets to, mixing flour and water into a paste for me to stickily gum the thin coloured strips together again, loop through loop, liberally pasting my apron and gluing my fingers to the newspaper spread on the table in front of me in the process.

One cold windy day the following spring, Lily comes running out at playtime shouting,

"Ere! It'll all be over soon, wot did I tell yer? Me Mum phoned up las' night an' sez us'll be back 'ome before long she reckons. Not that I 'as a 'ome to go back to mind, cos she got bombed aht agen. She's livin' rahnd me Nan's now so suppose I'll 'ave to go there too. Wot 'bout you?" She turns to me, standing open-mouthed, unable to understand her frantic gabbling. "Go back same as the rest of us won't yer? Even the Yanks is all gorn to finish off the Jerries, so they say, an' won't be back, so that's it, innit?"

But Rose understands. She takes my hand and we walk to the furthest end of the playground. Rose's round face is unhappy and she says,

"Funny, I never thort've you goin' back to Lund'n but if the War's nearly over and Lil's right... I won't arf miss you Louise. You will write to me won't you? Promise?"

That long-forgotten time, oh ages ago, when I'd worried about going back to London for good, to strange new schools, comes flooding back as I gaze at Rose.

Before I can answer Mr Murray blows the going-in whistle but this time we don't run to line up but walk slowly, heads down, staring miserably at the ground.

"My sister said once she'd ask Aunty if we could stay when the War's over but that was ages ago, I don't know if she did. I'll find out and tell you tomorrow."

Chapter Nineteen

It was the oddest thing. 'Going back to London' began to take on special significance and instead of being just one of scores of little girls and boys at the Village School, me and the Vaccees became strange, almost glamorous beings. The furthest most of us had ever been was Exeter, some twenty-odd miles away, or Totnes in the other direction. Now all of a sudden we were going *hundreds* of miles away and never coming back.

Once or twice I caught Rose looking sideways at me, as if I'd turned overnight into somebody quite different. And yes, in a way things had changed, although I didn't honestly know what leaving for good really meant. Santie did. She had asked Aunty May about staying on and Aunty said if it was up to her we'd stay for ever but it was for Mum and Dad to say and don't get your hopes up too much.

Once the News was official Mum got instantly on the phone demanding our immediate return, the sooner the better.

"Mummy sends her love to you both," Aunty said, coming into the back room where Santie was staring into space and I was colouring in my Big Picture Book. "I'm afraid she and Daddy want you both back as quickly as possible. Which is only to be expected after all, it's right you should be with Mummy and Daddy. Santie dear, don't look like that, I did ask if you could stay but – anyway, I'll tell you what I've been thinking and with any luck your Mum might agree."

I glanced up to see Santie's sad little face fix its gaze on Aunty May.

"Now," Aunty squashed herself round in front of the wireless, sitting down heavily. "You know it's not all over yet, don't you? Your Uncle and I don't think it's right for you two to go back before the War's properly ended once and for all so what I'll do is... "

"But Aunty," I interrupted, "Lily says it's all over bar the shouting and her Mum's coming to fetch her in a couple of weeks to go to her Nan's."

"Yes, Pieface, you're right, the War in Europe *is* over. But some of Our Boys are still fighting in the Far East and that's not over yet, not by a long chalk. So what I'm thinking is if I ask Mummy whether she'd let you stay at least for another couple of months and if it goes on any longer we'll have to see. Santie! Don't smother me like that!"

For she had jumped up and flung herself at Aunty May, knocking my coloured pencils on the floor, making the old wireless rock on the sideboard as Aunty's chair knocked back against it.

"Oh Aunty, would you? Please-please-please? D'you think she will? Let us stay I mean? Shall I write and ask? Shall Louise write too? Oh I'm so happy! Can we go to the Pictures this afternoon? Me and Lou?" Santie crouched down to pick up my pencils, winking at me, shining-eyed.

"*I'll* do any writing that's got to be done for the moment – be better to write first anyway. Do you really want to go to the Pictures today? Seems a shame, a nice sunny day like this. Why don't you go into the Village, wouldn't that be more interesting, see your friends? You two and your Pictures! All right then, if you must. Go to the first performance, I'll do you a sandwich to take with you. Mind you come straight back for tea. Have you looked to see what's on?"

THEIRS IS THE GLORY it was called. Coming out in the hazy sunlight – I never understood why it wasn't pitch dark outside like it was inside the cinema – and waiting for the bus home, Santie said,

"That's just about the gloomiest flick I've ever seen. Talk about joyful! Did you cry? I did and the woman next to me was SOBBING!"

Cry? I couldn't work it out, found nothing to cry at. There was dust and tanks and shouting, people throwing fir-cones at each other which went BANG and fires and at the end some women fell down holding fir-cones and there were more BANGS and the film finished.

Rounding the corner of the lane, Santie suddenly stopped dead and pointed towards the house.

"Look, look!" There's a flag flying in front of the house!"

Running up to the gate we stopped and stared. In the centre of the front lawn, next to the paving that formed a circle round the stone sundial, which had 'The Kiss of the Sun for Pardon, The Song of the Birds for Mirth, One is Nearer God's Heart in a Garden, Than Anywhere Else on Earth' written on a flat stone at its base, Uncle Fred and Gramps had set up a great big flagpole and high on the top a large Union Jack hung limply in the heavy air.

We beamed at each other.

"Isn't it lovely?" I said, "I love flags, don't you?"

"Oo yes, pity it's not fluttering out though, still it might... oh no, I don't believe it!" Santie had pushed open the gate and was staring at the long rope tied round and round the flagpole.

"What a swizz. I bet that's Gramps, look Lou can't you see? He's used our skipping-rope to put up his rotten flag. After we'd hidden it so well and all, the mean old thing, spying on us all this time. I shall tell Aunty."

Santie had found this long piece of old washing-line behind the White House about a year ago and we used to tie one end to the gate at the top of the drive. Then grasping the other end, Santie would turn the rope as I jumped in and out, chanting, 'One potato, two potatoes' or 'One-two-three, Mother caught a flea', each turn of the rope keeping time with my thudding feet. When I tripped up and was Out, Santie and I changed over, reluctantly on my part, for the heavy rope was tiring for small arms to turn. Santie didn't seem to mind though; she said arm exercises were good for swimming and turned the rope without complaint for as long as I could keep up.

At the end of each game we'd wind the rope up and Santie hid it carefully under a blackcurrant bush near the top gate. She arranged bits of leaves and earth on it and no one could see it just walking down the path. I think she was right and Gramps had used our skipping-rope out of spite for there were tons of old bits of washing-line in that nasty cupboard in the kitchen which would have done just as well.

Of course Grandad strenuously denied all knowledge of our skipping rope, saying it was a bit of old rope he found chucked under a hedge. Aunty said it was possible Gramps had done it on purpose but perhaps this time he had found the rope like he said. Santie tried to argue, pointing out anyone could see it wasn't just any old rope, but it was no use, his word against ours; Aunty said forget it now, it's done and she'd find us another piece to use. It didn't have the same 'feel' though, and after a couple of turns we abandoned it.

A few days after this Mum rang up and Santie and I, from under the gate-legged table on the landing, heard Aunty's side at least and could guess Mum's replies. Aunty didn't raise her voice at all, was pleasant and reasonable and when she said,

"Yes Grace, I do understand how you and Jim feel but it'll be a terrible wrench for us after all these years and I can't thank you enough for seeing it my way."

Santie dug me hard in the ribs so I gasped, squeaking in pain; shushing me by clapping a hand over my mouth, we heard Aunty say,

"Yes, dear I'll tell them and we'll see what the News is by then. Give our love to Jim, wish him better from me. Bye-bye dear – oh, there's the pips. Bye-b – oh, she's gone."

Putting the receiver back she called up the stairs,

"I know you're listening up there – Mummy says you can stay till the end of July and then we'll see…" But Santie was already half-way down the stairs, laughing and holding out her arms to Aunty May.

One warm summer evening Aunty May, Uncle Fred and Gramps, Santie and I put on our Sunday best, called for

Captain A (I'd never seen him before), Mrs A, Edward and Elizabeth and we all made our way towards the Church but instead of going in we turned up a narrow path just beyond and went up on The Downs by Dainty Bank. There was to be a pageant, with lights and fireworks, put on by the grown-ups and some of the older children so I wasn't in it this time. It was lovely to see light streaming out of cottage windows and on the railway we could hear the station's gaslamps popping as we walked by.

Music and lights, people dancing, singing, a great big bonfire high on the steepest slope. When this was lit wave upon wave of cheering echoed round and happy faces stared upwards, as, with a whoosh and loud bang a blaze of coloured stars burst overhead. For the very first time I was watching fireworks and their magic has never left me.

When it was nearly over, Aunty said it was time to go "as those children are dropping with tiredness", Uncle Fred lifted me up on his shoulder and, despite Aunty saying anxiously,

"Oh Fred, be careful, are you sure she's not too heavy for you?" he insisted on carrying me home.

A couple of days later Edward saw Santie in the lane and ran to tell her that after we'd left somebody put railway detonators in what was left of the bonfire and they'd gone off in a man's face and he was taken away in an ambulance to the hospital. When he returned to the Village he was quite blind.

Chapter Twenty

"It'll be August I reckon, the way things are going," Aunty said, looking up from her 'quick glance' at the *Daily Mirror* one rainy morning towards the end of July. She had been sadly packing our things into boxes and trunks for some time now although no summons had come from London.

"It can't drag on much longer. It'll be a relief to get back to normal again, no more rationing, but still... " Her voice tailed off and she rustled the pages noisily. "Well, this won't get the baby a new bonnet," she said briskly, getting up and starting to clear the plates off the table. "What are you two going to do today? Not the Pictures again surely and it's too wet to go swimming, you'll be wetter out than in! There are one or two things I need from the Village if you feel like a walk – nothing urgent, it's up to you."

"OK, why not? Suppose I have to take Old Trouble too?" But Santie was grinning at me so that was all right.

That evening dead on seven o'clock the telephone rang. Snatches filtered through to us listening behind the half-open hall door.

"A week or two at the most, so they say... Yes, of course you want them with you... Yes, for the holidays, I'll expect them... D'you mean Christmas or what? Are you coming down then?"

By the middle of August it was all well and truly over and though Aunty tried several times to keep us for a while longer Mum's mind was firmly made up and home we would go.

So one early September day two forlorn children were hustled through smoky, smelly Paddington by a harassed and tactless mother, grumbling how she'd had to leave Daddy at home, him being ill again it was this heat, didn't do anybody any good, and Next Door being good enough to keep an eye on him.

So now she'd got to cope on her own coming halfway across London to fetch us and that mountain of luggage, I thought it was coming on later and what May gave you that great marrow to bring home for I'll never know, it's not as if we like marrow anyway. Come on now, stop dawdling, we haven't got all day.

"When are we going back to Aunty's?" Santie asked as we dragged along by Mum's side.

"You can forget all that, you're home now for good," Mum snapped unkindly. Santie's face crumpled and we both snivelled, holding each other's hands tightly.

The following summer we returned to Devon for a short holiday but it wasn't the same. Without realising it we had adjusted to London life, new schools, friends; we had grown away, as Aunty feared we would.

Later that year Uncle Fred had a stroke which left him partly paralysed. He died in 1947.

"I call it morbid," Mum said quietly to Santie as they stood among the sombre black group on the path after Uncle's funeral, looking at his headstone. The small marble slab was the shape of a propped-up open book with Uncle's details carved on the left side of the 'page'. The other side was blank.

"Poor old May," Mum continued, glancing round but Aunty was deep in conversation with Reverend Dyer. "Every Sunday for the rest of her life she's going to walk past that blank stone knowing full well one day her name'll be on it."

And barely three years later it was.

UNCLE FRED 1869-1947

AUNTY MAY 1896-1950